MEDITERRANEA

ANASTASIA MIARI

MEDITERRANEA

Life-perfected Recipes from Grandmothers of the Mediterranean

ANASTASIA MIARI

For my family,
Greek and Italian

ORIGINS [8]
A NOTE FROM BEHIND THE SCENES [12]
MEDITERRANEA [14]

THANK YOU [248]
MINI GUIDE [251]
ABOUT THE AUTHOR [252]
INDEX [253]

SHARING [18]

COMFORTING [70]

FEASTING [140]

TREATING [198]

Origins

Six years ago, I made the decision to move back to the Mediterranean. A decade in London and even longer in the drizzly North of England had not managed to shake my Greekness. If anything, as with many diaspora Greeks trying to connect with their identity in less sun-kissed climes, I became more Greek. Sunday lunch in my London house share was observed as religiously as it is at my Greek yiayia's home on my island of Corfu. I served up *yemista* or slow-cooked lamb *yiouvetsi* with orzo as opposed to the classic Sunday roast, always with a hefty slab of feta on top of tomatoes that tasted like they'd never seen the sun. It was not exactly my yiayia's cooking, but it just about conjured the flavours of her white-washed outhouse kitchen on the days when I needed her most.

This book is the book I wish I had back then, but not just because the recipes instantly transport me to a land where olive trees stand testament to fertile earth and cloudless days. This is a passport to classic dishes and some lesser-known traditional recipes of the Mediterranean basin that will bring warmth to any kitchen. Transcending just food, it is a tome of lessons to live by, gleaned from women equipped with the experience of a lifetime.

After *Grand Dishes* and *Yiayia*, this is the third book I've written inspired by grandmothers. I've been buoyed by the sheer number of people that write to me about my own yiayia. People on the other side of the world in Melbourne, New York City, Toronto and countless other faraway places are cooking yiayia's lentils, conjuring the scents of her Greek island in their own homes. From this, it's clear to me that my passion project has the power to unite, inviting people to share in my culinary heritage in a deeper, more meaningful way.

I'm so moved every time my two-year-old daughter picks up my books and leafs through the recipes, pointing to her favourite dishes or otherwise delightfully exclaiming 'YIAYIA!' every time she lands on a picture of her great-grandmother, a squinting smile mirrored back at her, eyes the same colour blue. I am honoured to be able to pass these recipes on to Calypso.

There's something to be said for legacy and the written word. For centuries, the stories and legacies of women like my grandmother have not been recorded. We all know history was written by men, but the real history of our food culture has been forged by the women I feature in the pages of these books. It makes a lot of sense to me, therefore, to continue to document their stories and preserve the recipes and culinary skills that they have perfected over their lifetimes for generations to come.

Mediterranea is my love letter to the Mediterranean – the land I grew up in and the sea that drew me back home.

Being from Greece, having lived in Sicily and the South of France, and now being married to an Italian, I vouch not only for the Mediterranean diet being 'the healthiest diet in the world' (credited for our long life expectancy and low rates of disease) but also for our lifestyle. After many years in England, I chose to come back to blue skies, an affordable local farmer's market, last-minute plans and sharing meze with loved ones. While our dishes vary from region to region, the culture around food is shared across the Mediterranean basin in the countries I visited, from France, Spain and Italy to Greece, the Balkans, the Levant and North Africa. In addition to enjoying a collection of largely plant-based recipes that can effortlessly become household staples, I hope you will glean some of the secrets to a fulfilled and happy life from the pages of this book. Writing this book has been a journey of discovery and culinary reconnaissance that has become an expansion on my own heritage and further cemented my belief that we must look back in order to move forward in a meaningful way.

This is not a book about what it's like to be old. It's about how we can choose to live.

The lessons are simple but, when applied, powerful. The food is made with basic ingredients but the produce bursts with freshness and flavour. Let this be an edible baton to inspire future generations to live in the style of a Mediterranean grandmother. Beyond cooking the vibrant dishes within these pages, move your body, swim in all seasons and walk in nature, even when your knees creak. Surround yourself with friends and connect with your neighbours and elderly family members. Share food. Eat a little of what you fancy, usually with a glass of wine. And for goodness' sake, nap more.

A Note from Behind the Scenes

It is virtually impossible to have a grandmother send me a recipe or dictate the cooking process of a certain dish over the phone. The result is never the same because these women have never measured ingredients in their life. Their interpretation of a 'drop', 'dash' and 'sprinkle' is always different to my own. It's therefore imperative to be militant about the entire process. For every recipe in this book, I've cooked with the grandma in question, showing up to her home with a set of weighing scales and a measuring jug and insisting – much to their amusement – on weighing and measuring out the entire process. These recipes are written down on the go and then, once I get home, are tested multiple times.

The photography, too, has also always happened on site at the grandma's homes, just before a meal is served, fresh from the oven, or else during the cooking process. Under normal circumstances, photoshoots for cookbooks usually require a team of cooks, testers, stylists and photographers with assistants, not to mention a studio. One dish might be made multiple times in order to capture the perfect shot. I wouldn't dare ask my yiayia to make the same dish for me more than once so, understandably, Marco and I had one chance to get each of these photos right. We were the producers, stylists and creative directors of each shoot and the grandmothers' kitchens, dining rooms, gardens or final sunlit corners of rooftops became our studios. We used the utensils, crockery and tableware that was available to us, always from the grandmothers' homes.

It was often chaotic and quite hilarious, having to improvise with what was available to us. Sometimes the meal would have taken so long to make that we'd miss our window of natural light and have to resort to flash as the sun set. On other occasions, the entire family would pile into the kitchen to watch, comment and nibble at Marco's artfully placed mise en scene. For our cover shoot, Yiayia gave away a whole tray of yemista to my aunt's family to eat, thinking we had finished with it. In Naples, we had an entire table fall apart as we attempted to move it across the room to catch the perfect shaft of sunlight beaming through the kitchen door. Sorry Nonna Italia, that was not our finest moment.

Mediterranea

When I set out to write this book, I wanted to create a beautiful compendium that would represent the very best of the culture of the Mediterranean basin. Having travelled extensively already across the region and lived in Italy, France and Greece, I wanted to both celebrate all that we hold dear but also champion places and dishes that might not instantly come to mind when we think of the Med. Of course, I included classics like *spaghetti alle vongole* that capture the feeling of a summer's day by the sea in Positano (page 161) or those, like the cassata *Siciliana*, that are reminiscent of my time living among the chaos, drama and Baroque architecture of Palermo (page 237) but I cast my net wide.

In this book you'll find stories and recipes from the grandmothers of Spain, France, Italy and Greece (the usual suspects), but also the dishes of matriarchs from Tunisia, Algeria, Morocco, Lebanon, Palestine, Turkey, Cyprus, Croatia and Slovenia. It was very important to me to show the diversity of Mediterranean cuisine in this book and even in the more 'obvious' countries, I sought out dishes like Insalata di Cedro (page 38) or Soupe au Pistou (page 129) that were regional and told the story of a specific place. I hope you'll agree that I've struck a nice balance between classic, widely known dishes like lasagne on page 194 (I really am willing to bet this is the best lasagne recipe you will ever make) and new, exciting meals that may well establish themselves as staples in your own repertoire (the Tunisian Lablebi on page 83 and Omek Houria on page 57 are now popping up weekly at my dining table).

Eating my way across Greece for my last book, *Yiayia*, I realised I wanted to delve deeper into my own heritage as a woman of the Mediterranean. Beyond the delicious, no-frills meals and wholesome produce, it's the way we eat that made me want to write a book dedicated to the entire Mediterranean basin. The way those Greek grandmothers threw open their crochet-curtained doors to me, welcomed me as a member of their family and fed me to bursting inspired me to seek out more similar experiences.

While the dishes you can find across the Med vary – from hot and spicy harissa-spiked dishes in North Africa to sumac-sprinkled recipes towards the Levant and punchy, garlic-packed plates in France – the way these women eat and, in turn, live, is essentially the same. The traditions of *cucina povera* (see page 62) and making what little you have go a long way is a resounding theme in these pages, as is the concept of 'picky eating' and sharing a small bite before or between meals (see page 37).

Many of the women in this book lived through abject poverty in their formative years. As with my own yiayia, meat for them has always been a treat, appearing at Sunday lunch or on feasting days. We no longer have the luxury of denying climate change or the impact that eating meat has towards it.

This book is packed with vegetarian and vegan options, purely because the grandmothers of the Mediterranean have always eaten in this way.

Above all else, I've found that hospitality and an impassioned – and, quite frankly, pathological – need for sharing food is really what unites all the women in this book. It's a trait I have inherited and this book is a manifestation of my need, as a Mediterranean matriarch of the next generation, to feed you all the love and joy I devour daily.

A NOTE IN MY DEFENCE

I would have loved to have travelled to every single country that sits on the Mediterranean basin but budget and time constrictions along with certain political situations meant a few were missed. In order to get around this, I asked chefs from some of the respective countries I wasn't able to make it to, to give a dedication to their grandmother in the form of a written recipe. I was so moved to read their words and feel very honoured to be able to share their grandmothers' recipes with you in this book. One day, I will make it back to Bethlehem and Beirut!

SHARING

BREAKFAST

I can't say I have the fondest memories of my own Yiayia Anastasia's breakfasts, which would consist of a mug of warm milk with bits of soggy bread and a globulous poached egg floating in it. I'm certain the bread was just Yiayia thriftily trying to make use of stale slices that would otherwise end up on the floor of the chicken coop. She would plonk this down in front of me and sit across the kitchen table, side-eyeing me as I glumly poked the contents of the mug with my plastic Little Mermaid spoon – all while she went about scaling fish, plucking dead birds or butchering the latest little lamb that had met its fate. It was a far cry from what those beyond Greece think of as a 'Greek breakfast'. In the 1990s, creamy whipped yogurt, honey and walnuts were seemingly reserved for tourists.

Greeks are generally not known for their breakfasts, often reaching instead for a cigarette and a silty coffee brewed in a brass *briki* in the morning. Yiayia, like many yiayiades across the country, starts her day with two *friganies*: simple wheat rusks (dry as a rubber flip flop left out in the sun) that she dips into her coffee. The frugality of yiayia's breakfast might have a lot to do with the fact that Greece was an extremely poor country until she was well into her adulthood.

Expanding beyond Greece, the 'continental breakfast', now a staple at most hotels across the world, was coined by the British in the 19th century. As they are wont to do, the British lumped the countries of Europe and the Mediterranean under one banner, 'the continent', in which everyone supposedly ate simpler, more frugal breakfasts than the hefty English portions of bangers, bacon and eggs.

While I do love a 'full English', the assumption that all Mediterranean breakfasts consist of slices of pink, slightly wet ham, yellow cheese and watery yoghurt does the entire region a disservice. Travelling across the Mediterranean for this book, I've indulged in a diverse set of dishes to start the day off right. Each country has its own breakfast traditions that vary hugely. Preferences will depend on whether you have a sweet tooth in the morning, liking to begin the day with a sugar hit, or not.

SOME LIKE IT SWEET

Beginning with the obvious: pastry. These are a prerequisite for breakfast across France, Spain and Italy. In Marseille, I ate the best *pain au chocolat* of my life, scoffing it as I drove precariously up Provençal mountain passes to visit grandmothers Maryse and Bruyère. It had the crispest, flakiest and most dense outer layering, wrapped around a rich chocolate centre. In Mallorca, the first thing I picked up at a local bakery en route to the abuelitas of the island was an *ensaïmada* – a sweet spiral pastry that is light and airy despite being cooked with lard (the *ensaïmada* has been awarded protected food status in Europe).

To the south of the Mediterranean, Algerians enjoy pancakes oozing with local honey for breakfast. Lamia, my half-Algerian foodie guide in Tunis, made me pancakes (page 32); something between a feather-light French crêpe and a squidgy British crumpet, the 'pancake with a thousand holes' is traditionally eaten with your hands, dipped into a warm sauce of melted butter and honey, a joyously sensorial start to the day.

I can't begin to cover the expanse of sweet treats offered at an Italian breakfast table but, suffice to say, it's not one most would consider 'healthy'. My Italian man – embarrassingly – still eats the breakfast he consumed as a child in the 1990s: a bowl of milk, in which he dips his gocciole (teardrop-shaped chocolate chip cookies). He's not the only Italian that prefers to kick-start the day with a sugar high. When I lived in Palermo, I first experienced the chaos of an Italian 'bar': the pre-9 a.m. mayhem of what seems to be a hundred elbows nudging each other out of the way to get to the glass-fronted bar containing cream-filled *cornetti* (pastries) and cannoli exploding with sugar-spiked ricotta and candied fruits. This has now become a morning ritual on every trip I take to Italy, the only difference being the variation of sweet treats on offer according to the region.

When I visited my friend Marcello to cook with his grandmother, Nonna Cece in Ragusa, his partner Nikos was tasked with picking up breakfast from the *pasticceria*. He returned with *cornetti* spilling thick pistachio cream and topped with a crisp layer of icing (frosting). In Italy, there's really no such thing as a 'plain butter croissant'.

In Puglia, I took comfort in shortcrust pastry filled with custard, while in Naples, my eyes widened at the utter delight of biting through my first *sfogliatella*. While I will forever prefer a savoury breakfast to the above sweet options, I will make an exception for this pocket of creamy ricotta tucked into a multitude of crispy, tracing-paper-thin layers, traditionally baked with lard. Despite having tiny flecks of candied orange running through it, it was cooling rather than cloying in the thick Neapolitan summer heat.

ON THE SAVOURY SIDE

Being half English, I tend towards an umami brekkie. While sweet hits the spot when I'm travelling and allowing myself a little indulgence, I'm a firm believer in a protein-packed breakfast with eggs at its heart. For this reason, the majestic spread put on by Esma in Turkey is a breakfast menu I now turn to again and again (see pages 22–29). Cheese- and potato-filled crispy *börek* parcels, fried peppers dipped in garlic yoghurt, a vibrant herby salad, sumac-sprinkled eggs atop greens, sesame simit bread and a selection of dried fruit, nuts, jams and tahini paste weighed down the table at Esma's when she invited me for breakfast. All the makings of an epic brunch.

This isn't an exception in Turkey. It's a standard breakfast you're served across the country, with variations on the eggs, the salad and the type of *börek*. In Urla, at chef Osman Serdaroglu's restaurant and boutique hotel concept, I woke up to a breakfast of bubbling fried eggs served in the pan they were cooked in, sizzling in the rich butter of the region. In addition to this, local cheeses, cream, honeycomb and a bowl of cucumber and tomato salad, simple yet bursting with flavour.

While travelling across Turkey, waking day after day to a table so full of various dishes I could barely decide what to eat first, I was amazed at how different attitudes towards breakfast can vary from one region of the Mediterranean to the next. Greece is a neighbouring country and yet our breakfasts pale in comparison to the kingly proportions of the Turkish. The only common denominator is the traditional coffee, though I found the Turkish to be more partial to sweet tea in the mornings.

Elsewhere, in Tunis, a soul-enlivening chickpea (garbanzo) stew, *lablebi*, is often served for breakfast, topped with a poached or boiled egg. Alive with harissa, cumin and turmeric, this common Tunisian 'fast food' is served out of hole-in-the-wall establishments across the country. While I cooked the dish with grandmother Latifa and ate it at home in the company of her family (see page 83), locals are known to head to canteens across the city as early as 5 a.m. to get their fix. If you're ever in Tunis, Weld Hnifa is the place to get yourself a steaming-hot bowl of *lablebi*. Grab a traditional clay bowl, break up your own bread and place it in the bottom of the bowl, then line up for a man to ladle out the spicy stew, *Oliver Twist* style. This century-old stalwart of the city is where Tunisians go to feed a hangover. I've placed the *lablebi* recipe in this book in the 'Comforting' chapter, but I do recommend trying this one for breakfast, particularly on a crisp winter morning.

SHARING 21

Esma's Kahvaltı
Turkish Breakfast

There's nothing quite like landing into a country starving hungry and being treated to the kind of hospitality you get in Turkey. Esma is the first grandmother I met on the Turkey leg of my grandma odyssey and when I arrived at her house on a Saturday morning, she offered to make me a Turkish breakfast.

Esma lives in Selçuk, a historic town in which majestic storks nest on the walls of the ancient city of Ephesus. As I stroll to her home, the enormous birds pass mere centimetres over my head, seemingly oblivious to the farmers' market and its bustle below. I'm proud of my local *laiki* (market) in Athens, but I have to admit that Selçuk's market puts it to shame. It sprawls across an enormous square and pours into the alleyways that come off it. Fruit and vegetables like purple flowering artichokes are in abundance. Spices call out at me from other stalls, the hot red of paprika and sultry aroma of sumac demanding my attention. Then there's the guy selling sesame-topped *simit* (Turkish circular bread) of all variations behind the glass of his cart, one of which is filled with chocolate. It's a surprise I make it to Esma's house at all.

When I do arrive, Esma is already busy at work at her flower-patterned kitchen table, preparing the breakfast of a Sultan for us. She insists that, in life, hard work pays off and in order to work hard, we must eat a breakfast that energises us. Cue a table heavy with tahini, jams, eggs, *simit*, fried dried chillis, yogurt, *börek* and salad. It is enough to feed an army and this, apparently, is a normal breakfast here in Turkey...

The following recipes make up the components of Esma's Turkish breakfast, along with homemade jams and *simit*. Make all of the following for brunch and it should feed up to six guests generously.

Esma's Kavlama Biber
Red Pepper Crisps with Yogurt and Garlic Dip

Biber is 'pepper' in Turkish and *kavlama* means 'to heat up'. This surprisingly entertaining addition to Esma's breakfast is perhaps my favourite, thanks to the crispy red peppers that vary in degrees of spicy from pleasant tingle to 'that just set my mouth on fire'. It's the Turkish breakfast equivalent of Russian roulette. Fried to a satisfyingly crunchy consistency, the peppers become dippable crisps (chips) that we scoop up garlicky yoghurt with, cooling our mouths down after a particularly hot one.

SERVES 4

INGREDIENTS

300 g (10½ oz/1¼ cups) yoghurt

3 garlic cloves, crushed

40 g (1½ oz) salted butter

1 tablespoons olive oil

25 g (1 oz) dried sweet sivri peppers (you can find these in Turkish delis or use a dehydrator on any sweet red peppers)

1. Whip the yoghurt in a bowl with a whisk, then stir in the garlic and set aside.
2. Heat the butter and oil in a frying pan over a medium heat and fry the peppers for 1–2 minutes until they begin to crisp up and take on a darker hue.
3. Remove from the pan and served alongside the yoghurt for dipping.

Esma's Cingen Pilavi
Cheese and Herb Salad

Though *pilavi* means 'pilaf' and denotes a rice dish, *cingen pilavi* is actually a salad with no rice in it whatsoever. The crumbled cheese curds resemble rice and are the key component of the dish. It's a recipe native to the west of Turkey, where Esma hails from, and in true granny form, it was popularised as a means to use up the curd that was a by-product when making butter. It's fresh, aromatic and full of flavour, thanks to the combination of herbs and spring onion used. I particularly love Esma's addition of nigella seeds at the end, a powerful antioxidant to kick-start your day.

SERVES 4–6

INGREDIENTS

190 g (6¾ oz) cheese curds (or crumbled feta or ricotta salata)

2 tomatoes, diced

1 cucumber, diced

handful of dill, fronds and stalks finely chopped

handful of rocket (arugula), finely chopped

handful of parsley, leaves and stalks finely chopped

2 small green (bell) peppers, finely diced

2 spring onions (scallions), finely diced

100 ml (3½ fl oz/scant ½ cup) olive oil

20 good-quality black olives

1 teaspoon nigella seeds

1. In a large salad bowl, combine the cheese, tomatoes, cucumber, dill, rocket, parsley, peppers and spring onions, then top with the olive oil and black olives. Don't worry about seasoning the salad as the olives and cheese should be salty enough. Finish with a sprinkling of nigella seeds.

Esma's Cigar Börek
Potato and Ricotta Filled Pies

A crispy, crunchy pastry roll filled with salty cheese (if you can't find ricotta salata, feta is a great replacement) and potatoes, the cigar *börek* defies my expectations of a *börek*, in that it isn't oven baked at all. A bit like a Greek pita (pie), the *börek* is ubiquitous across Turkey, Greece and the Balkans. It was probably proliferated by nomadic Turks and records have proved that *börek* was being made in the region way back in the 7th century. The term *börek* can be applied to many types of pies in varying shapes, from standard square slices and envelopes with a warm filling to spirals. Esma's is the first I've ever tried in cigar form but I'm all for it, especially as it's sizzled in a pan of oil for extra indulgence.

MAKES 15

INGREDIENTS

3 potatoes (about 300 g/10½ oz), peeled, boiled, cooled and grated

150 g (5½ oz) ricotta salata or feta, grated or finely crumbled

½ teaspoon sea salt

½ teaspoon ground black pepper

150 g (5½ oz) ready-made filo pastry

40 g (1½ oz) unsalted butter

1 tablespoon olive oil

1. Combine the potatoes, cheese, salt and pepper in a bowl and set aside.

2. Take a couple of rectangular filo sheets at a time and cut them up into obtuse triangles. You should get four triangles from one sheet by cutting it in half widthways (across the short side) and then each piece in half again across the diagonal. Don't worry too much, because as long as you have a triangle shape Esma's method will still work. Repeat until all the filo is cut into triangles.

3. Have a small bowl of water nearby and keep any filo triangles that are waiting to be used under a clean, damp dish towel to stop them drying out. Place a triangle of filo in front of you with the longest side of the triangle closest to you and the tip pointing away. Place 2 level tablespoons of the potato mixture 2 cm (¾ inch) from the bottom in a strip, leaving a 2–3 cm (¾–1¼ inch) gap at each end. Fold the bottom edge over the mixture once, tucking it in slightly, then fold in both sides (to close the ends) and continue to roll the bottom edge up into a neat cigar shape. Seal it by dipping a finger in the water bowl and lightly brushing the point of the triangle and smoothing it down to stick. Repeat until all the filling has been used up.

4. Heat the butter and oil in a wide non-stick frying pan over a medium-high heat, and, when hot and bubbling, fry the cigars in batches without overcrowding the pan. Using tongs, turn the cigars over after 2 minutes to reveal a golden brown side and keep turning for up to six minutes or until they're nice and golden all over. Remove them from the pan and place on a tray lined with paper towels to soak up the excess oil and cool slightly. Transfer to a serving dish and eat while they are still warm.

Esma's Otlu Yumurta
Eggs on Greens

This dish is spectacular in its simplicity, and I love that I can use up any wild greens or leftover herbs and spring onions (scallions) lurking in my refrigerator to make it. Esma throws her eggs together using a bunch of spring onions, but I've tested this with leeks and beetroot (beet) tops too and the result is resoundingly tasty using both variations.

SERVES 6

INGREDIENTS

60 ml (2 fl oz/¼ cup) olive oil

1 large bunch of spring onions (scallions), cleaned and chopped into 1 cm (½ inch) rounds (use all the onions, including the green tops)

1 green (bell) pepper, finely chopped

6 medium eggs

1 teaspoon sumac

sea salt and freshly ground black pepper

1. Heat the oil in a frying pan over a low-medium heat, then add the spring onions and pepper and fry for about 10 minutes until softened. Crack in the eggs and fry to your liking.
2. Season with salt, pepper and sumac.

'I grew up with a sick mother, so I learned to make breakfast very young. I had six siblings but five of them were boys, so from the age of seven I began to make breakfast, despite being the youngest of them all. The boys, of course, never cooked.

Here in Turkey, breakfast is the most important meal of the day. We have to work hard for anything we get in life. I generally believe that we get back what we put in, but without a good meal to power us on, we can't achieve what we set out to do. I don't just mean the men that go out to work and earn a living. Housewives have the toughest role of all in society. Raising a family is a job and it takes willpower to be able to mother. It shouldn't be underestimated. I am the mother of three girls and I'm so proud to have brought up these women. Girls are the helpers in a household, and they have so much strength. The power of women is not like that physical power that men possess. We have strength of mind.'

ESMA — B. 1942 — AYDIN — TURKEY

Sitti Malak's Za'atar Mana'eesh
Palestinian Za'atar Flatbreads

B. 1939 — GAZA CITY — PALESTINE

DEDICATION BY FOOD WRITER JENAN ASHI

Za'atar lives at the centre of every Palestinian table. No matter the time of day, you're almost guaranteed to find a small bowl of sesame-studded za'atar, coupled with another bowl of the freshest olive oil, ready to be orbited by its owners. For Palestinians, za'atar is a lifeline, a form of clinging to their heritage and centuries of history. Foraging the wild shrub has been banned since the 1970s, but this hasn't stopped Palestinians from using it at any given opportunity.

Za'atar *mana'eesh* are a brunch staple across the Levant, and no memory of *mana'eesh* is more distinctive for me than the one I ate in February 2006. It was on my family's first visit to Gaza in almost a decade, and we were greeted with love and abundance. We stayed with family, of course, and bunked with our cousins to make the most of our week-long trip of a lifetime.

During the week we were reunited with our family, and every single meal of the day was shared together. So many of them were cooked by my maternal grandmother, Malak Al-Borno.

Malak, meaning 'angel' in Arabic, couldn't be a more fitting name for the woman who liked beautiful things and had to be perfectly presentable, changing outfits and accessories after each prayer of the day. Malak, or Sitti, as we'd call her, wasn't known for her cooking. But she was taught the art of a good *man'ousha* (plural: *mana'eesh*) by her mother-in-law, who would bake pittas and other breads in a clay oven.

On a weekday morning on our late winter visit to Gaza, Sitti had decided to bake up enough *mana'eesh* to feed an army of children and grandchildren. The children sat at a low table in the living room, sinking our teeth into the fluffiest dough, crowned generously with za'atar and olive oil, and respectfully washed down with the sweetest cup of sage-infused black tea.

MAKES 8–12 FLAT BREADS

INGREDIENTS

625 g (1 lb 6 oz/5 cups) plain (all-purpose) flour

2 tablespoons granulated sugar

2 tablespoons dried yeast

pinch of salt

500 ml (17 fl oz/2 cups) warm water

250 ml (8 fl oz/1 cup) olive oil

165 g (6 oz) za'atar

sweet black tea, to serve

1. Preheat the oven to 250°C fan (520°F).
2. Put 250 g (9 oz/2 cups) of the flour, the sugar, yeast, salt and warm water into a bowl. Mix roughly, then cover and set aside for 10 minutes until the mixture has become foamy.
3. Add the remaining flour and half the olive oil, then mix again and knead gently for a couple of minutes until you have a soft dough.
4. Shape the dough into 8–12 balls and leave them to rest and cover with a cloth while you prepare the za'atar mixture.
5. In a small bowl, combine the remaining olive oil with the za'atar and set aside.
6. Roll each ball of dough into a 10 cm (4 inch) circle and top with 1½ tablespoons of the za'atar mixture, leaving a 5 mm (¼ inch) border around the edge.
7. Bake the breads on a baking sheet (you may need to do this in batches) in the oven for 6–10 minutes until the dough is slightly golden on the edges and the bottom and the za'atar is sizzling.
8. Serve warm with sweet black tea.

Lamia's Baghrir
Algerian Pancakes with a Thousand Holes

My brilliant guide to all things food in Tunis, Lamia, takes me on a tour of the Marché Central on my first day in the city to pick up ingredients for dinner. We pass row upon row of heavy branches of dates, dangling above our heads on fine twine and weave our way through market stalls piled high with enormous green olives and mountains of fiery harissa paste. Along the way, Lamia shares tidbits of Tunisian history with me.

Running food tours in and around Tunis, Lamia is an expert on the city's culinary heritage. I'm surprised to hear that Tunis was home to a high population of Italians less than a century ago. She points out that Tunis, while not recognised as such, is a gastronomic hub in North Africa because of the culinary influences that have passed through here. Tunisia has been a crossroads to many civilisations; the Phoenicians, Romans, Berbers, Arabs, French, Italians and Jewish communities all at one point settled here. Lamia herself is of Italian and Algerian descent.

In a nod to her Algerian roots, we make a breakfast staple together that has now become a favourite in my household. Nicknamed 'pancakes with a thousand holes', *bahgrir* could be the lovechild of a French crêpe and a British crumpet. Made without eggs or milk, they are thin, squidgy and dotted with holes that greedily absorb a warm butter and honey spread, making them a great vegan option (if you use vegan butter and maple syrup) for a decadent (albeit thrifty) breakfast.

MAKES 10–12 PANCAKES

INGREDIENTS

250 g (9 oz/2 cups) fine semolina (farina)

150 g (5½ oz/scant 1¼ cups) plain (all-purpose) flour

5 g (⅛ oz) dried yeast

1 teaspoon salt

1 teaspoon granulated sugar

650 ml (22 fl oz/2¾ fl oz) lukewarm water

40 g (1½ oz) unsalted butter (or 1 teaspoon coconut oil)

20 g (¾ oz) baking powder

butter and honey, to serve

1. Combine all the ingredients except the butter and baking powder in a bowl and use a hand blender to whisk everything together. Add the baking powder and blend for a good 30–60 seconds. Let the batter rest for 15–30 minutes.

2. Add 10 g (½ oz) of the butter in a large non-stick frying pan over a high heat, moving the pan to distribute the butter while taking care not to burn it.

3. Use a ladle to spoon some of the batter into the pan. Ideally, the pancakes should be around 2 mm (⅛ inch) thick. They're not thick, American-style pancakes, so use the batter modestly and allow it to spread across the pan. After around 20 seconds, holes should begin to appear on the surface of the pancake. Wait for the entire surface to be covered in holes, then use a spatula to remove the pancake from the pan. Place it on a warm plate or baking sheet to retain the heat while you continue with the remaining batter. After making four pancakes, Lamia runs her frying pan under the tap to cool it down and avoid burning the pancakes. She then adds another knob of butter before continuing with the rest of the batter.

4. Serve in the traditional way with butter and honey, melting the butter and adding a couple of spoons of honey (to your taste) before dipping the pancakes into the honey butter blend. I find this also pairs well with nut butters and jams.

'I'm Algerian from my father's side of the family. When I was a young girl and our Algerian relatives would come to stay, we would all eat this in the morning with tea or a milky coffee. It's a traditional breakfast served with copious amounts of honey. Algerians have a sweet tooth, and we like to start the day off with something saccharine.

I may live in Tunisia, but I have always had a sense that I am Algerian inside. We Algerians are very frank and we're known for having short tempers. We're very direct and we don't dance around an issue. If we have something to say we will come out and say it. I have inherited this trait from my father, and I have to say it is something I am grateful for. I don't believe in false politeness – I think if there is something you have on your mind, you might as well come out and say it rather than letting it sit and become passive aggressive over time. In relationships, not just romantic but with friends and family too, it is always better to be honest.'

LAMIA — B. 1969 — TUNIS — TUNISIA

PICKY EATING

While most diners in the western world are now becoming au fait with sharing plates menus at restaurants, it should be pointed out that in the Mediterranean basin, 'picky eating' – as I like to call it – is more than just a trend. It is a way of life. I grew up on the Greek ritual of 'meze'. My lunches and dinners have always been a chaos of arms criss-crossing over a diverse spread of light bites, served *gia* to *trapezi* (for the table), no single dish belonging to one individual but rather an array of small plates for everyone to serve each other, share and comment on. Try to order your own plate in Greece and you're at the mercy of your fellow diners. The dish will likely land far from your own seat at the table, being passed around for others to pick at before it arrives before you, half-devoured.

In my years living in and travelling across the breadth of the Mediterranean to cook with grandmothers, I have found this mode of eating repeated again and again. Think *aperitivo* in Italy, sharing cheeseboards in France, the Moroccan tea ceremony, tapas in Spain, meze across Turkey, Lebanon, Palestine, Cyprus and Greece. It's a unifying factor of dining in the region and one of the things I'm most proud of in our culture. We know how to share, and we take pleasure in doing so, partly because of how obsessed with food we are and how much joy we draw from simply talking about the food that we're partaking in, but also because of the strong culture of hospitality that we all share. Picky eating also requires a lot less effort, with a focus on great-quality produce served simply, allowing the ingredients to shine – another touchstone in Mediterranean cuisine.

Each individual country's relationship with picky eating varies, though we can give the Romans some credit for their ritual of *gustatio*, the practice of opening up their appetite (*aperitivus* in Latin) before a meal with a light bite accompanied by a slosh of honey wine. Alcohol has long been linked to this style of dining. The merchants and labourers of the Middle Ages in Constantinople (modern-day Istanbul) had a penchant for a glass of *raki* and a salty hunk of cheese or cured seafood meze before heading home for lunch. This tradition has been repeated across Greece and Cyprus, travelling with the Romioi (native Greeks) expelled from the 'Polis' (Istanbul) and resettling with them across the Greek islands. In a similar vein, the sherry-drinking Andalusians covered their glasses with a 'tapa' of ham or chorizo to prevent fruit flies from getting to the sweet contents.

Some of my most treasured memories from my trips have been the moments in which we've been welcomed into homes and served a selection of specialties from a specific region, the food working as an edible ice breaker – forever my favourite way to get people talking. On my trip to Mallorca for this book, my Spanish friends Lucia and Claudia hosted us on a sun-drenched terrace overlooking a deep, velvety sea, its crashing waves framed by olive trees. Fat slices of chorizo and giant Spanish olives were served next to slick silver sardines in the tin and a plate of creamy burrata-topped toast garnished with orange zest and slithers of salty anchovy fillets. I couldn't have wished for a better lunch or a more scenic backdrop. Elsewhere on the island, Margarita served us a Coca de Verduras (page 19), potato crisps (chips) and a cold *cerveza* in a frosted glass retrieved from the freezer as I tried to decipher her dialect, while Maria towered zesty tomatoes and crisp peppers onto hefty slices of toast for her Pa amb Oli (page 16), two recipes I'm so pleased to be able to share with you in this book.

Concetta's Insalata di Cedro
Sicilian Citron Salad

Nonna Concetta, or 'Cece' as her family call her, is waiting for me in a sun-drenched courtyard under the shade of a lemon tree when I arrive in the morning at her home in Ragusa. Orange blossom drips on us as we dine on a feast of *cornetti* (croissants) filled with cream and pistachios and cannoli spilling out sugary ricotta with every bite. It's a true Sicilian breakfast – a saccharine feast to fuel a mighty five-hour cook-a-thon in which Cece and her granddaughter show me how to make some dishes specific to the beautiful Baroque city of Ragusa.

The hilltop city where she grew up is on the south-east coast of the island and is almost fairytale-like in its beauty. It rises up from the landscape, built on wide limestone and undulating in varying shades of yellow, pink and blue. Laundry blows above my head, strung up on ancient washing lines that run across the narrow alleyways. I don't need to wonder what it might have been like for Cece growing up here, as very little has changed in the way of architecture. The city is a protected UNESCO World Heritage Site and will be here long after we're all gone – the thought is humbling, knowing that something of Cece's youth will be here forever.

Made with thick-rinded cedro (citron), one of the original varieties of citrus, it is a refreshing, flavour-packed and perfectly balanced dish. The zing of the cedro flesh and the subtle sweetness of its rind combines with a salty kick of anchovy and the punch of chilli to create the ultimate salad. I have also tried a summer version of this recipe (as cedro is ripe and ready over winter) using sweet honeydew melon and I loved the result.

Eat it on its own or, as Cece demands, with plenty of bread to mop up all that oil. This salad is the star of the show and needs no other pairing.

SERVES 4

INGREDIENTS

1–2 cedro (citron)

6 anchovy fillets in oil

½ bunch of parsley, leaves finely chopped

2 spring onions (scallions), white parts finely chopped

½ fresh or dried red chilli (dried chilli/hot pepper flakes, in a pinch)

100 ml (3½ fl oz/scant ½ cup) olive oil

1. Using a vegetable peeler or a very sharp knife (if you're as handy as Nonna Cece), peel the waxy skin from the cedro, leaving a very thick rind.

2. Chop the cedro into 2 cm (¾ inch) chunks. The key ingredient here is the pith, so if your fruit has a lot of juicy inner segments, set those aside to use in something else and use the rind.

3. Combine all the ingredients in a bowl and serve immediately.

'Ragusa Ibla – the old town – was all I ever knew for the first 14 years of my life. It's only a 20-minute drive away from the beach now, but as a child, I never saw the sea. I was one of six children and we didn't have a means to get to the beach so I didn't see it until my sister married. I would ask my mother, 'What does the sea look like? What's it all about, the "sea?"' and she'd respond, "Oh, there's just a lot of water there."' I couldn't picture it at all.

We would leave the town to walk to a nearby patch of land my father owned and there we'd grow vegetables and bring them back up to the house. Otherwise, my siblings and I kept ourselves entertained with games that we would play in the courtyard of the house. We'd take away an old, loose tile and throw walnuts into the hole. Those of us who managed to get our walnuts in, would win the loser's walnuts.

When I was 10 years old, my family put me to work. I began working on textiles, including a technique unique to Sicily called sfilato, or 'drawn thread', in which we would pick out sections of the thread within linen or cotton textiles to create a detailed pattern within the fabric. Fabric production has been very important to the island since medieval times and it was something a young girl could do because the technique we used needed a very fine, delicate hand. I was so good that by the time I reached 14 years old, the lady I worked for invited me to Paris to work there. My parents refused and demanded I stay near them. That was very disappointing to me, I would have liked to have seen France.'

CONCETTA — B. 1933 — RAGUSA — SICILY

Margarita's Coca de Verduras
Mallorcan Vegetable Tart

SERVES 12 SLICES

INGREDIENTS

1 butterhead (bibb) lettuce (about 150g/5½ oz), trimmed and finely chopped

2 teaspoons flaky sea salt

2 small leeks, finely chopped

6 spring onions (scallions), finely chopped

1 small bunch of parsley, leaves finely chopped

1 teaspoon ground black pepper

1 teaspoon smoked paprika

1 garlic clove, crushed or grated

150 ml (5 fl oz/scant ⅔ cup) olive oil

2 small tomatoes, thinly sliced

handful of pine nuts, lightly toasted

FOR THE PASTRY

½ teaspoon bicarbonate of soda (baking soda)

100 ml (3½ fl oz/scant ½ cup) cold water

100 ml (3½ fl oz/scant ½ cup) olive oil

50 g (1¾ oz) lard or unsalted butter, at room temperature, cut into small cubes

300 g (10½ oz/scant 2½ cups) plain (all-purpose) flour, plus extra as needed

When I first met Margarita, I swiftly realised that my level of Spanish doesn't quite cut it when it comes to Mallorquin grandmothers. Margarita speaks a dialect that sounds closer to Portuguese than it does Spanish, and I couldn't quite wrap my head around the words she used throughout our cooking process. Thankfully, her grandson, Jaume, a local chef, was at hand to translate.

From the very beginning of our day cooking together, Margarita is warm and welcoming. She tells me she's used to cooking for strangers and that the dish we're going to make is a very typical dish that she has been making since she was a child. Every Mallorcan is familiar with *coca de verduras*, a crisp, thin-based tart weighed heavy with plenty of vegetables. Toppings can vary, and I'm intrigued by Margarita's use of butterhead (bibb) lettuce in this particular recipe. The coca is described as a flatbread or pizza as it isn't yeasted at all. It's best enjoyed with a beer and a couple of other small plates and would make a great addition to a picnic, packed lunch or garden party spread.

1. Preheat the oven to 200°C fan (425°F) and line a roughly 38 x 25 cm (15 x 10 inch) baking tray (pan), preferably cast iron, with baking parchment.

2. Put the chopped lettuce into a large bowl, add 1 teaspoon of the salt and massage it into the lettuce to break it down a little. Add the leeks, spring onions and parsley to the bowl with the remaining teaspoon of salt, the pepper, paprika, garlic and olive oil. Stir to combine.

3. Next, make the pastry. In a separate bowl, combine the bicarbonate of soda with the water, olive oil and your choice of fat. Stir to combine and break down the cubes of fat a little.

4. Add the flour bit by bit, combining with your hands and rubbing the cubes of fat into the flour to break them up. Do this until it comes together into a soft, pliable ball that doesn't feel sticky. Add more flour or water a teaspoon at a time if the dough is too wet or dry. You are going to press this into the tray rather than roll it, so you don't want it to be too stiff.

5. Place the dough in the centre of the prepared tray and pat it down to flatten it. Begin to spread it out across the entire base of the tray with your hands, pressing in with your fingers and pushing the pastry outwards until it reaches the edges in a thin, even layer. Prick it all over with a fork, then bake on the bottom of the oven (not on a shelf) for 5 minutes. Placing it on the bottom of the oven will help the base crisp up.

6. After 5 minutes, when the base is a little more firm, remove the tray from the oven and cover the pastry evenly with the greens, then spread the slices of tomato on top. Return to the bottom of the oven and bake for 10 minutes, then move to the top of the oven for a final 5 minutes, or until the pastry is golden and the topping is nicely cooked and slightly charred in places. Remove from the oven and top with the toasted pine nuts, then serve hot or cold.

'I've reached my nineties, but I don't particularly feel very old. Thankfully, I can still get around and take care of myself as well as the children and grandchildren. I have a life of hard work to thank for that. I was born into a family that wasn't hugely wealthy and so, like many children at the time, I was sent to the estate of a rich French family here in Mallorca. That way, my parents could ensure I would be well taken care of, but it also meant that I couldn't go to school. I was nine years old when I left to work on the estate and I was terrified to leave my mother, but I have to say that, in the end, they took very good care of me and treated me as their own daughter. I learned a lot there about the land and about cooking, which I have loved ever since.

When I was married, aged 22, I moved back to Sóller into this big house, which I've lived in ever since. Beneath the floor that I occupy on my own now used to be the kitchen, which would heat up the entire house. We'd sit at the dining table and put coal in a brasero, a metal heater, that was underneath it to keep us warm. I couldn't tell you exactly how old this house is but certainly more than 200 years. At that time, we were able to take in poor children from a much less affluent part of the island and feed them. That was very standard practice back then. I would cook for my family and so many more every day.

Sóller was a very wealthy part of Mallorca because it has always been surrounded by olive groves, which the Arabs brought with them and the Spanish continued to cultivate once they were gone. It's also a port town, which wealthy French merchants made use of, so the houses are made of stone and very stately. They're beautiful, with lots of details like the tiles here in this house. More importantly, they were made to last.

It was in that first job that I learned to make coca de verduras. I've been making it for over 80 years now, so we can say I've become an expert. The key to this recipe and my ultimate tip is to use a hardy iron tray to make it and to cook it on the lowest level of the oven with the top and bottom setting on. You want the vegetables to caramelise and the dough to cook at the same time. No one wants a soggy dough. You want it to come out crispy like a tart.'

MARGARITA — B. 1932 — MALLORCA — SPAIN

Nezahat's Turkish Artichoke and Broad Bean Stew

This is an elegant dish that works as a starter (appetiser) or a side dish, and can be eaten cold as a salad, too. I love its versatility and the way the dill and lemon uplift the whole thing.

I met Nezahat's great-nephew, chef Osman Serdaroglu, at a pop-up dinner in Athens. When we got chatting about my obsession with the recipes of matriarchs, he insisted I make the journey to Turkey to meet his great-aunt. Osman runs a Michelin-star restaurant and boutique hotel concept in the lush region of Urla, but he credits his great-aunt for teaching him all there is to know about Turkish cuisine.

Nezahat has published her own cookbook and, in true Turkish granny style, has made multiple dishes for me to sample on my arrival, despite my insistence that she not go overboard. This artichoke dish is the one I plump for as a representation of the experience I have in Urla, because everywhere I go in the region, I see artichokes. Fields and fields of them expand out to the horizon on the drive from Selçuk to Urla, purple flowers saluting the sun. At the local market, women wearing brightly covered scarves around their heads sit and gossip while cleaning the prickly outer leaves off and dumping the tender hearts into vast buckets of water, ready to be bagged and sold to home cooks like Nezahat.

SERVES 4

INGREDIENTS

3 lemons

6 globe artichokes

350 g (12 oz) broad (fava) beans (fresh or frozen)

150 ml (5 fl oz/scant ⅔ cup) olive oil

1 large onion, finely diced

4–5 garlic cloves, finely chopped

1 teaspoon salt

300 ml (10 fl oz/ 1¼ cups) water

1 tablespoon caster (superfine) sugar

2 tablespoons finely chopped dill

1. Nezahat can buy globe artichoke hearts ready-prepared at her local market, but if you're not as lucky, start by half-filling a large bowl with cold water and squeezing in half of one of the lemons (keep the other half to daub your artichokes with as you prep them). This is to stop them browning.

2. Take an artichoke and begin by snapping back the tough outer leaves until the pale yellow ones are exposed. Use a sharp knife to trim the top off, pare down any remaining leaves at the base and peel the tough outer skin from the stem. Use a teaspoon to remove and discard the fibrous 'choke' in the centre of the heart. It should look like a shallow artichoke chalice. Cut it in half or quarters lengthways and place in the bowl of lemon water. Repeat with the remaining artichokes.

3. If your broad beans need their skins removing, do this now by blanching the beans for 2 minutes in boiling water, then draining and rinsing under cold water before using your fingers to slit the wrinkled outer skins and squeeze out the green bean from inside.

4. Gently heat the oil in a wide lidded pan over a low heat and fry the onion and garlic with the salt for 10–15 minutes until soft and translucent, but not golden.

5. Add the juice of the 2 remaining lemons, the water and sugar. The liquid should almost cover the artichokes but not quite, so add a splash more if needed.

6. Drain the artichokes in the bowl and add them to the pan. Cook on a low simmer with the lid on so that they steam and don't brown. This should take about 20 minutes.

7. Ten minutes before the end of the cooking time, add the broad beans, cover and bring to the boil – cook for 5–10 minutes until the beans are al dente. As soon as the artichokes are soft, gently remove them from the pan with a slotted spoon. Set aside and keep warm while you stir in almost all the dill. Spoon into bowls and top with the artichokes and a final sprinkle of dill.

'I learned to cook from my mother. She was always cooking and always sending food to the neighbours. Now I seem to have followed in her footsteps, and I make these huge portions of food and send it round to all the neighbours. I am very proud of my own cookbook, which contains many of my mother's recipes but also dishes I've picked up on my journey through life. The title is Hands and Eyes because it reminds me of a story I once heard about Atatürk, the founding father of the Republic of Turkey. He once asked his cook what the secret was to his marvellous food. He wanted to dissect the recipes and what went into each dish to make it so special. The cook replied, 'I don't know, sir, I just measure with my hands and my eyes.' It felt very fitting because this is how most great cooks prepare their food. They feel it.'

NEZAHAT — B. 1940 — ISTANBUL — TURKEY

Matilda's Krumpir Salata
Dalmatian Potato Salad

After a morning of feeling like a pinball being batted between throngs of tourists in Split's Medieval old town, I'm relieved to finally breathe again as I drive down the glistening coastal road to Matilda. She lives in a blink-and-you'll miss it village, nestled into a wild and Jurassic-feeling landscape between Split and Dubrovnik. This is the Croatia I came for. It is humbling to sit at Matilda's table, watching her peel searing-hot potatoes with her bare hands without so much as a flinch as she recounts the story of her life.

This potato salad may be simple, but because Matilda dresses the potatoes while they're still hot, they soak up the sweet acidic tang of the vinegar, resulting in an incredibly flavourful side dish. I like to think of it as an edible metaphor for the resilience and strength Matilda has shown over the course of her life. Peeling a hot potato is nothing in the face of what this woman has encountered in her long lifetime.

SERVES 6

INGREDIENTS

1 teaspoon flaky sea salt, plus extra as needed

6 large waxy potatoes

½ small onion (red or regular), finely sliced into half-moons

4 tablespoons extra virgin olive oil

2 tablespoons good-quality red wine vinegar

freshly ground black pepper

1. Bring a large saucepan of water to the boil, add the salt, then boil the potatoes in their skins for 20–25 minutes until soft. Drain, then peel off the skins while the potatoes are still hot. Matilda has magic, life-worn hands that mean she can do this quickly and barely feel the heat. I ask if we can wait until the potato has cooled and she advises strongly against this, as the potato absorbs the dressing and flavours of the vinegar and olive oil much better when warm.

2. Chop the warm potatoes lengthways into 5 cm (2 inch) thick slices and place in a bowl, followed by the onion.

3. Combine the oil and vinegar in a small bowl, then pour over the potatoes evenly. Season to taste with a sprinkling of salt and black pepper.

'We eat our potato salad with plenty of vinegar because when I was a young girl there were many vineyards in this region. We don't let anything go to waste so, of course, if wine would turn into vinegar, we would use it in our cooking.

My aunt taught me how to cook because I lost my mother when I was very young. I was just five years old when she died. I don't remember a huge amount, but I do have a memory of waiting impatiently at the gate of our house with my two sisters and brother for my mother and father to return home from the doctor. When I saw their figures coming towards us, I had a sense that it would be bad news. I don't know how this was because I was so young, but this is a memory I have held onto for over 80 years. I just knew inside me that it would be bad news.

On her deathbed, my mother asked my father to bring me and my siblings to her so that she could see us one last time before she died. We were lined up at the end of the bed by my father and my mother took her last breath with us all there beside her. It was the time of the Second World War and there was so much instability, even here in the countryside. At my mother's funeral, they had to call in a priest from one of the neighbouring villages because our own priest had been murdered by partisans.

I was 19 years old when I married Filip. We met one day when I was carrying water back home from the well. I would walk nearly 2 km (1.2 miles) to go and collect water for the house from the fresh-water spring. We'd wash our clothes there and then bring water back to the village in a wooden canister on our backs. This was always the woman's duty. On one of these days, I saw Filip and fell in love. He was so tall and very handsome, with bright blue eyes. He had just returned from Slavonia (a region in Croatia), where he'd been living because the partisans had moved themselves into our village and taken over his house. When we married, we moved back into the family home, but they would only allow us to use the upstairs. The partisans continued their occupation of the home, which had a disastrous effect on our lives. I fell pregnant and on the night I gave birth, they had a raucous party downstairs. I was so stressed and felt unsafe. I'm convinced this is why my baby boy didn't survive the birth. I almost didn't pull through myself, and a priest was called, followed by a doctor who had to come out multiple times in the week to save my life.

Filip's brother lived with us at the time of this event and I believe he was never the same after that night. It affected him to the point of mental breakdown and I took care of him for the rest of his life. I prayed to Mother Mary because I didn't have a mother of my own anymore and my faith gave me the hope I needed to continue to live out my years. My daughter has brought a lot of happiness to my life and now my granddaughters, too. They look after me. It's not just a comfort; it is a joy to have them.'

MATILDA — B. 1933 — PODGRADE — CROATIA

Houriye's Omek Houria
Tunisian Carrot Dip

On my first day in Tunis, I meet Houriye with her grandson, Mamou, at their local market in La Marsa, a coastal city on the outskirts of Tunis. Together we hand-pick the ingredients for our lunchtime feast and I see Houriye and Mamou work their way through the merchants' stalls, feeling the vegetables, sniffing at parsley and joking with the stallholders, who planted, grew and harvested the vegetables themselves.

As I observe them together it strikes me how important it is that they are able to connect with the food that they eat in this way. The carrots we choose for our salad aren't packaged in plastic; they're loose, a bit knobbly and still have their tops firmly intact. It's one aspect of eating that many of us in the Mediterranean take for granted: our proximity to our food.

Together we make *omek houria*, a carrot 'salad' that I would say is closer to a dip, akin to Greek *melitzanosalata* (aubergine 'salad'). Punchy with fresh garlic and a healthy dollop of harissa, this is an incredibly versatile dish. Houriye, Mamou and I eat it with chunks of fresh tuna on top, but it also makes a brilliant vegan addition to a selection of meze bites or as an accompaniment to roast chicken or grilled fish. It's bright, light and has become a summer picnic essential for me and my family.

SERVES 6

INGREDIENTS

8 carrots, peeled and chopped into 2.5 cm (1 inch) rounds

1 teaspoon sea salt, plus extra to taste

1 tablespoon harissa paste

2 tablespoons olive oil

2 tablespoons white wine vinegar

1 teaspoon caraway seeds, pounded in a pestle and mortar

1 garlic clove, crushed

1 bunch of parsley, leaves very finely chopped

crusty bread or pitta bread, to serve

1. Bring a saucepan of water to the boil and cook the carrots for 15 minutes, then add the salt and continue to cook on a rolling boil for a further 5 minutes, or until the carrots are completely soft. You can also choose to steam the carrots (retaining more of the nutrients of the vegetable), but ensure they're soft enough to mash after steaming. Drain and allow to cool before the next step.

2. While the carrots are cooling, combine the harissa, oil, vinegar, caraway seeds and a pinch of salt in a jug (pitcher) or small bowl, stirring until they come together.

3. Once the carrots have cooled, use a pestle and mortar (as Houriye does) or blitz the carrots into a purée in a food processor, then transfer to a bowl. Combine the puréed carrot with the harissa dressing, garlic and parsley.

4. Serve with crusty bread or pitta bread.

'My life and my relationships with other women in my life have been hugely affected by my relationship with my mother, in that I never had one. Things were very different back then and my mother was married at 13 years of age. She was very young, but her family deemed it acceptable and necessary. My father was fairly well off and was able to take care of her financially and so it was arranged that she would marry him, though he was more than twice her age. Her father decided that it would be that way and as the daughter, it was her duty to obey him.

My mother became pregnant with me almost right away, but she hated what was happening to her and to her body. When I was born, she refused to breastfeed me and wouldn't even pick me up. We had goats on my father's farm at the time and a baby goat had been born in the same month as me, so they nourished me with the milk of his mother. I have heard all this second hand, but I believe it to be true because a couple of years later, my brother was born and she reacted in the same way to him, too. She then ran away and abandoned us completely.

Tunis is a small place, so news eventually made its way back to us that she remarried and had a new family, whom she stayed with and gave birth to more children whom, I imagine, she loved and nurtured because the time was finally right for her. The sense of abandonment I felt as a baby has never left me.

My father remarried but my brother and I were never loved by any mother figure in our lives. We were left to take care of each other and so, in a way, I made many maternal sacrifices for my younger brother. I became the maid for a Jewish doctor and moved into his home in order to secure an education for my brother. While I worked as the maid, my brother was trained to be a nurse and the doctor's assistant – in this way, he was able to better his life.

As for me, I never went to school. It was normal back then not to receive an education. Schooling in an institutional sense only began once Tunisia was colonised and, even then, it spread across communities very slowly. My education was in the land, in farming and in taking care of the home. I knew nothing different and learned to cook from a very early age as a result of this.

I may be exceptionally harsh with my daughter, but I am very proud of her. She studied hard, found a good job in an institution and is in a happy marriage with brilliant and beautiful children of her own. The most transformative moment in my life was performing Hajj and seeing the house of God in person. It made me appreciate the beautiful things that have happened to me, despite my difficult beginnings.'

HOURIYE — B. 1939 — TAZOGHRANE — TUNISIA

Jana Lala Hada's Moroccan Preserved Lemons

DEDICATION BY CHEF NAJAT KAANACHE

To me, North African cuisine without preserved lemon is like the Oreo cookie without its white cream filling. The lemon is naturally zesty and is preserved using a brilliant, artisanal method without the use of any machines. Adding preserved lemon to a dish will turn something good into something amazing. It lends the dish an intense flavor without turning it sour because the tanginess is gone and what remains is the rich, pure taste of lemon.

What exactly are preserved lemons? They are lemons that are preserved with salt and stored for months in their own juice before you being used. They're quick and easy to make and will add a sweet and sour magic to many dishes and even cocktails. In the Middle East, Asia and North Africa they are added to salads, meat and fish recipes as well as to sauces, purées and mousses. Anything that could use a little lemon, really.

If you preserve your lemons immediately after harvesting them, you can enjoy them for the rest of the year: they will keep for a long time.

MAKES 12 PRESERVED LEMONS

INGREDIENTS

3 kg (6 lb 10 oz) flaky sea salt

2 tablespoons caster (superfine) sugar

12 organic lemons, scrubbed

1. In a bowl, thoroughly combine the salt and sugar.
2. Using a sharp knife, carve a deep 'X' into the top and bottom of each lemon. Sprinkle the cuts with the salt mixture.
3. Spoon a layer of the salt mixture into the bottom of one large or several smaller sterilised jars. Place the lemons on top and fill up with more salt mixture until the lemons are completely covered. Because you are using sugar you can store the jar(s) in the refrigerator during the fermentation process. If you don't have enough space in the refrigerator, place them in a dark, cool spot.
4. Leave to ferment for 4 weeks, shaking the jar(s) every day to make sure the salt and sugar are evenly spread around.
5. The lemons are ready when they take on a paler tone and are soft.

There is a guardian angel by my side, and that guardian angel is my grandmother. The woman who taught me how to make the best biscuits (cookies), breads and casseroles. She carried me like the wind and took me with her through the countryside in search of experiences so that I would never forget her.

My grandmother, no matter how old I am, will always be worried: 'How are you? Did you eat? Are you OK?' She is someone I could always depend on emotionally, especially at mealtimes. I have always enjoyed simple food made with her hands, imbued with love and honesty. She always listens with an open heart, is a great friend, a protective leader and is forever concerned that I eat the best of the best. This is how I learned to celebrate local products, made with joy. She taught me to take advantage of seasonal ingredients, give them life and rescue them for other recipes and seasons.

Jana was a genius. During the summertime, she would preserve the entire garden, using herbs, flowers, vegetables, roots and any type of edible fruit. She would preserve them by curing, burning and smoking, creating unique flavour profiles that you would struggle to find nowadays. She also had an incredible pantry of botanicals and used herbs, spices, honey and natural ingredients to cure all types of illnesses. She was an instinctive and powerful herbalist with a dark room full of unique jars, each one with different preserves. It was like a bank, in which she would save her precious summer bounty for the winter months ahead.

I love you, Jana.

Thanks to those times together, cooking for hours in the morning to make lunch, I make a living cooking and remembering the flavours you gave from your soul to the world. My entire career is built around letting people know where I come from with our traditions, cuisine and culinary techniques.

When I close my eyes and see your own eyes shine back at me, they give me strength to continue a legacy that I learned from you. My perfect grandmother, from earth I send you my only request: do not forget me and continue to be by my side from heaven.

Jana, I love you.

LA CUCINA POVERA

The term *cucina povera* (kitchen of the poor) originated in rural Italy, but this style of thrifty eating has been adopted by the matriarchs of kitchens across the Mediterranean. In its simplest sense, *cucina povera* used the best of what people had available to them to create hearty, filling meals that could power a working day in which most of the tasks to be accomplished were labour-intensive and manual. This meant using ingredients grown locally and seasonally and making use of the entire animal, if a family was lucky enough to afford meat or reared their own livestock.

Before 'zero waste' was a trend, grandmothers across Italy and the rest of the Mediterranean basin were using the milled husks of their wheat or dried lentils as chicken feed. Meats were cured to keep a family going throughout the winter, hence prosciutto and other cold cuts. *Biscotti* – a staple in most Italian nonnas' homes – were famously baked twice to ensure they would last longer. On my trip to Turkey, grandmother Ayten told me she still uses ash from a wood-fired oven instead of bicarbonate of soda (baking soda) for her Kalburabasti (page 223), an ingeniously thrifty baking alternative that's long fallen out of use.

Many of the grandmothers I've cooked with for this book came of age in the 1940s. In Italy and its European counterparts like southern France, Spain and Greece, *cucina povera* became increasingly central due to the depressed post-war conditions. Elsewhere, in Croatia and Slovenia, the need to make use of what limited produce was available lasted right the way up until the break-up of Yugoslavia in the 1990s. Most of the recipes I have gleaned from the grandmothers in the latter two countries are great examples of delicious dishes that were born of necessity.

A main ingredient used in this type of cooking is bread. Cheap to produce and a key component of a meal that guarantees to fill the belly, a loaf of bread can go a long way. A uniting element of the cuisine across the Mediterranean basin and something I discovered on my great granny odyssey for this book is that over many lifetimes, our resourceful matriarchs have invented delicious ways of using up stale bread that might otherwise go to waste, like a soul-firing stew from Tunis or an afternoon pick-me-up from Mallorca.

Elsewhere in the book you'll find dishes made with *horta* (page 170) and *cicoria matta* (page 88), wild greens repurposed for consumption with a squeeze of lemon and a dash of olive oil. While you might not be able to find the exact same greens beyond Greek or Italian borders, I find my yiayia's way of cooking *horta* works just as well with beetroot (beet) tops, dandelion greens, amaranth greens and Swiss chard (silverbeet). Yiayia is an expert forager and will often point out wild greens on the roadside or sprouting in abundance all over my garden in Corfu, rolling her eyes and blaspheming at me for bypassing such a valuable source of nutrition. Raised on an island occupied by Italians during the war, yiayia and her siblings were forced to survive on weeds that are now à la mode in fine dining establishments across European capitals. It just goes to show how the humblest ingredients can shine if treated with love.

Maria's Pa amb Oli
Mallorcan Tomato and Olive Oil Topped Sourdough

Driving to Abuela María's home, I pass through fields full of flowering almond trees and citrus orchards with blossoms that give off the sweet scent of spring. Her home is full of intricately embroidered textiles that she has poured hours of her time into crafting, from chair covers to traditional linen curtains that hang from her windows. While we put together a simple lunch of *pa amb oli*, which literally translates to 'bread and oil' in the Mallorquin dialect, María lets me into the realities of island life and how traditions were born of necessity here.

Pa amb oli is usually eaten with unsalted Mallorquin bread that is made using the husks of the wheat. I prefer a salted, tangy sourdough so (contrary to what María would advise!) I like to make this one with a crusty loaf of that. It exemplifies what I love most about dining in Spain – there's a focus on simplicity and an abundance of flavour.

The best way to eat this is in company. Serve with Spanish olives, a decent jamón and cold beer.

SERVES 4

INGREDIENTS

4 slices of good-quality sourdough bread (can be a few days old)

3 ripe tomatoes

1 green (bell) pepper, thinly sliced

1 white onion, thinly sliced

2 tablespoons good-quality capers

olive oil, for drizzling

salt

1. Toast the bread lightly if it is fresh.
2. Chop one tomato in half and smush the inner side of one half onto one side of the toasted bread so that the juice seeps into in. Repeat for all four slices, then sprinkle with salt and douse with olive oil.
3. Top the slices with the green pepper, then thinly slice the remaining tomatoes and add those too, along with the onion and capers. Finish with another good glug of olive oil and a pinch of salt.

'I eat pa amb oli every evening for dinner. It's my go-to for something easy because, let's face it, housewives traditionally have a lot of work to do and the faster dinner is to prepare, the better. It's in our tradition to eat this here in Mallorca and it's one of the dishes that came about purely because the island was once very poor.

We would make the bread without salt because salt holds onto humidity and the island is very humid, meaning the bread spoils faster if it's salted. It's the produce and ingredients you add to the bread that add all the flavour. Of course, now you can add any selection of ingredients to pa amb oli, but I make a very simple version with seasonal produce I find around the village. Llubí is actually famous for capers, so these always feature. The key to a good pa amb oli is a healthy amount of good-quality olive oil.

Living on an island means that we have often had to make use of what we have. I worked making footwear all my life because I came from a poor family and, before tourism was an industry, Mallorca earned its keep with the production of shoes. We would use the rubber from old tires to create the soles of shoes here. We had to be inventive and resourceful because we're cut off from the mainland. The Mallorquina shoes are famous all over the world and I'm proud that they originated here because of our resourceful nature.

If I have any tip for life, it's to work and to try to keep oneself busy. I embroider in my spare time and I have crafted so many beautiful pieces. To put your time into creating something tangible is quite a satisfying thing, whether it's a meal for family or a hand-crocheted curtain.'

MARÍA — B. 1945 — LLUBÍ — MALLORCA

COMFORTING

MY YIAYIA ANASTASIA

I am the namesake of my Yiayia Anastasia and, along with her pronounced nose and sharp angles, I've taken on a lot of her qualities, for better and for worse. Yiayia is a complex woman, born of a time in which most of Greece lived in poverty. Being one of the eldest of 10 siblings, she was forced to work from eight years old and didn't go to school, famously biting the teacher's hand when the government at the time introduced a law that required children to attend night school, at the minimum. Despite never having learned to read or write, she has a mental bank of hundreds of poems that she recites from memory, dropping them at random over mealtimes or else when we're hanging out in her white-washed alley, watering her flowers or drinking Greek coffee together.

The term 'no filter' very much applies to yiayia. She is whip-smart and the funniest person in the family, with a quick wit that has absolutely no mercy. Embarrassingly for me, she will often sniff out a person's insecurities and, when she's feeling particularly devious, will prod and poke at them no end. She has no issues with telling my friends how much chubbier they look this year compared to last year or listing my shortcomings as a woman to the guests I host on my annual retreats in Corfu. I cannot describe the utter mortification I felt when, at my wedding dinner, yiayia took to mocking my new Italian mother-in-law's friends aloud, demanding I translate what she was saying to the confused and nervous glances of the well-coiffed Milanese signoras. The beatings with my pappou's leather belt, her slipper or an extra-whippy olive branch that I received from her as a child will always be preferable to yiayia's verbal bullying.

Writing this, I'm beginning to think I may well have what psychologists call 'Stockholm Syndrome'. As I said, yiayia is a complicated being. Under the bravado, wicked laughter and characterful facial expressions that have yielded a beautifully lined face, is a sensitive person that has great aptitude for reading her audience. In another time, under other circumstances, I'm sure yiayia would have made a great actress or dictator. She is an orator, someone who demands attention and holds it. Parallel to the performer runs a deeply passionate and emotional persona. Her fierce love manifests itself physically into crippling handshakes and breathtaking goodbye hugs.

On my wedding day, as is traditional, I chose to get ready at yiayia's house in the small Corfiot village home I grew up in. Hundreds of my friends from all over the world piled into her tiny alleyway as yiayia served them Greek coffees, finally having reason to bust out the 'new' glassware and crockery that had been boxed up in the back of her wardrobe for 40 years. That morning, two things confirmed the true nature of my wild and unyielding yiayia.

When I stepped into her living room, I saw that she had dressed the table herself, laying out a silver and gold shimmering spread of baklava, chocolate-dipped koulourakia biscuits and individual wrapped chocolates and sweets atop a gold embroidered tablecloth. At the heart of the table, beside the obligatory bottles of ouzo, Cognac and Metaxa, yiayia had placed a framed picture of Pappou. In her own small way, she had thought to place her husband, and my grandfather (lost to us in 2009) in the centre of all the action of the morning. No words were spoken, but I felt how terribly she must have missed Pappou's presence on that day.

I will forever be brought to tears at the memory of yiayia, her sisters and daughters singing to me that morning. In Corfu, it's tradition to sing 'the wedding song' to a new bride as she prepares to meet her husband at the church. I was having my hair done as yiayia burst into song, her shaking hand on my shoulder and my 85-year-old Theia Stamatella's hand on the other declaring, *'Today the sky is shining, our daughter is taken away. Please take care of our bride, love her and never upset her. Take care and celebrate her like a beautiful pot of basil, flaunt her.'* The emotion in yiayia's breaking voice, the trembling hands that kept absent mindedly patting my shoulders as they shook and the conviction with which she sang will never leave me.

Like many women of her generation, yiayia lived through great hardship, yet persevered. She raised a family and then raised her children's children too. Well into her old age, she still plants and harvests her own vegetables by the moon's cycle, makes her own olive oil and cooks a meal daily, even if it's just for her own pleasure. To me, she is the very essence of a Mediterranean matriarch; bright, bold and earthy. I will revere her and honour her great enthusiasm for life until my dying day.

Anastasia's Mosharosoupa
Beef and Orzo Soup

As with most of my favourite dishes in this book, yiayia's beef and orzo soup is a one-pot job. She simply throws everything into a 70-year-old soup pot and allows the contents to simmer away on her simple gas stove while she goes about her daily business. Now that I have a child of my own to care for, I truly appreciate the power of a dish like this. Not only is it nutritious and hearty, it requires minimum effort and I can multitask while it cooks. This dish has always been a staple in our family. It has a lovely balance of sweet notes from the tomato purée (paste), balanced with the deep umami of the beef. Also, pasta. And which kid doesn't like pasta?

SERVES 4

INGREDIENTS

2.5 litres (85 1/2 fl oz/ 10 1/2 cups) water

500 g (1 lb 2 oz) bone-in beef (ask for beef soup bones or beef chuck from your butcher)

1 tablespoon salt

4 small waxy potatoes, peeled

1 large carrot, peeled and chopped into 1 cm (1/2 inch) thick rounds

1 small red onion, with a cross sliced into the top

1 celery stalk, halved

2 heaped tablespoons tomato purée (paste)

3 tablespoons olive oil, plus extra to serve

120 g (4 oz) orzo

feta and olives, to serve

1. Pour the water into a large saucepan, add the beef and bring to the boil over a medium-high, then cover and boil for about 15 minutes. Once it's really bubbling away, spoon off the foam from the top.

2. Next, add the salt, vegetables, tomato purée and olive oil and simmer over a low-medium heat with the lid just slightly ajar for 45–50 minutes until the soup has reduced.

3. Strain the soup through a fine sieve set over a bowl. Set the vegetables and meat aside and return the broth to the saucepan. Add the orzo and cooking according to the packet instructions. Make sure to check the texture of the pasta to ensure it's cooked to your liking.

4. Meanwhile, pull any tender meat away from the beef bones and chop the potatoes and carrots into smaller chunks. Add these to the soup when you're ready to serve. You can season again to taste at this point, but yiayia adds a wedge of feta to hers so tends not to add more salt.

5. Serve with a simple drizzle of olive oil alongside feta and olives.

Soula's Spanakorizo
Greek Rice and Spinach Risotto

SERVES 4

INGREDIENTS

1 kg (2 lb 4 oz) spinach (Soula insists it is always fresh and never from frozen)

160 ml (5 1/2 fl oz/2/3 cup) olive oil, plus extra to serve

4 large spring onions (scallions), trimmed and chopped into 1 cm (1/2 inch) rounds

2 large leeks, trimmed and cleaned, then chopped into 2.5 cm (1 inch) half-moons

1 bunch of dill, roughly chopped

2 large garlic cloves, green germs removed and roughly chopped

700 ml (24 fl oz/scant 3 cups) water

150 g (5 1/2 oz/generous 2/3 cup) medium-grain rice, such as karolina

1/2 teaspoon ground black pepper

1/2 tablespoon salt

1 chicken stock (bouillon) cube (optional – reduce the salt by half if using)

1/2 lemon, for squeezing

feta and bread, to serve

It's spring in Greece and wildflowers are in bloom over a lush blanket of grass when I arrive in the Peloponnese to cook with Yiayia Soula. We head past neatly preened olive groves to the local *laiki* (market) to grab the ingredients for our spanakorizo and I can tell right away that Soula is a force to be reckoned with. She has no issue being photographed in the village, posing for the camera as locals gawp at the sight of me and Marco the photographer, snapping away while Soula comically surveys the veggies in a performative fashion worthy of an Oscar. When people inevitably ask what we're doing, she's the first to explain that she's being featured in a new cookbook.

Back home, we cook spanakorizo in the dappled shade of the orange trees in her garden. I find Soula's method of washing the spinach – in an enormous vat with a hose pipe – hugely entertaining and will be trying this at home.

This dish is a kind of risotto, but in true Greek style, the vegetables are the star of the show and it's much less fussy to make than a traditional Italian risotto (who has time for all that hovering and stirring?). An entire bunch of dill added into our pot brings a fresh meadow aroma to the garden and we serve it with a hefty chunk of feta and a wedge of zesty lemon.

1. Start by washing the spinach. Place it in a large bowl of water with a splash of vinegar and wash well, roughly tearing it to pieces as you do so and removing any tough stalks. The vinegar will ensure you get rid of any little friends hiding in the leaves.

2. Drain the spinach and place it in a large saucepan over a medium-high heat. Cover and allow to steam for 10 minutes. Next, add the olive oil, followed by the spring onions, leeks, dill and garlic. Cook, stirring every so often, for about 5 minutes.

3. Pour in the water and the rice, followed by the salt, pepper and stock cube, if using. Cover and simmer for 30 minutes, stirring occasionally to stop the rice sticking.

4. Once the rice is tender, season again to taste and add a squeeze of lemon for a final zingy flourish. Served with a slab of feta, an extra drizzle of olive oil and plenty of crusty bread.

'Lots of people aren't aware that spanakorizo is an interesting combination not only because it tastes good. Spinach is difficult for the human body to digest, but the rice and lemon that we add to it helps the body to absorb the iron. My mother was an excellent cook, and she told me this many years ago.

I lived in America for most of my adult life but have returned to Greece for the weather and the good produce. I like to go to my local laiki every Thursday – it's an outing that happens ritually every week. I tend to also go for walks in the surrounding olive groves every day, leaving my brother, whom I live with, to sleep in while I get out and about to catch up with friends or start on the day's chores.

I find that what is most important in life is to keep moving. Even when things get tough, we must put one foot in front of the other and keep walking. I am a mother who lost her son and that was the most difficult thing I have ever had to endure. Somehow, I still manage to smile, make jokes and approach life with lightness. I have eight grandchildren, and I have kept myself happy for them. I think being grateful for what you have is so important. We can't control what will happen to us, but we can control how we conduct ourselves through it.'

SOULA — B. 1946 — PELOPONNESE — GREECE

Theodoula's Deconstructed Koupepia
Cypriot Mushroom and Courgette Risotto with Vine Leaves

SERVES 2

INGREDIENTS

6 vine leaves, in brine

600 ml (20 fl oz/2½ cups) water

1 tablespoon vegetable bouillon

50 ml (1¾ fl oz/3½ tablespoons) olive oil

200 g (7 oz) button mushrooms, finely chopped

2 courgettes (zucchini), finely chopped

1 white onion, finely chopped

1 garlic clove, finely chopped

4 sprigs of thyme, leaves picked

1 tablespoon tomato purée (paste)

150 g (5½ oz) peeled tomatoes (can be from a tin)

1 tablespoon granulated sugar

200 g (7 oz/scant 1 cup) arborio rice

1 teaspoon salt, plus extra as needed

100 ml (3½ fl oz/scant ½ cup) red wine

60 g (2 oz) unsalted butter (optional)

60 g (2 oz) Parmesan, grated

handful of chives, chopped

handful of parsley, leaves chopped

juice of ½ lemon

1 tomato, finely diced

freshly ground black pepper

Greek yoghurt, to serve

DEDICATION BY CHEF STAVROS GEORGIOU
This recipe was inspired by a traditional recipe made by my grandmother and its very strongly connected to the memories I have of her during my childhood. Upon finishing school every Friday afternoon, I would walk to my Yiayia Theodoula's house. Without fail, her fragrant koupepia (stuffed vine leaves) would be waiting for me on the table. The scent would fill the whole neighbourhood. It was a wonderful feeling of love reflected in a plate of food. As an adult, I created a variation of the recipe, which is now served with love from me to your plate, in memory of my grandmother and the flavours of her kitchen.

1. Preheat the oven to 140°C fan (325°F) and line a baking tray (pan) with baking parchment. Spread the vine leaves out next to each other over the tray. Cover with another piece of baking parchment and place a smaller tray on top, using it as a weight. Bake in the oven for 15 minutes, then remove and aside.

2. Meanwhile, pour the water and vegetable bouillon into a saucepan and bring to the boil, then set aside.

3. In a hot frying pan, sauté the mushrooms and the courgettes in the oil over medium heat for a couple of minutes, adding the onion and garlic shortly after, followed by the thyme. Once the onion is translucent, add the tomato purée, tomatoes and sugar, stirring to combine before following with the rice, salt and wine. Allow a couple of minutes for the alcohol to cook off before continuing.

4. Use a ladle to pour a little of the broth into the rice, stirring with a wooden spoon and waiting until the rice absorbs it before adding another ladle. Do this until you've used all the broth, stirring continuously.

5. Before serving, stir in the butter, Parmesan, chives and parsley, lemon juice and finely diced tomato then season to taste with salt and pepper. Serve with a dollop of Greek yoghurt and the crisp vine leaves on top.

Latifa's Lablebi
Tunisian Chickpea Soup

I have a lot of fun meeting Latifa, who lives on the outskirts of Tunis with her husband and daughter. Squeezed into her red and white colour-block kitchen over a bubbling pot of spiced chickpeas, she and I clumsily communicate with my poor school-level French, but it's OK because her husband – who is Tunisian of Italian descent – is keen to flex his Italian language muscles. This proceeds to be rather hilarious when I ask (in Italian) if they had kissed at any point before their marriage. With a shy smile and a shake of her head, Latifa responds with a furiously wagging index finger, 'No!' while her husband shrugs, winks at me and says 'certo' (of course).

What I'm surprised to learn is that Tunis was home to an enormous Italian community prior to the end of the Second World War, during which many were ousted by the French and threatened to be thrown into jail for being allied with fascists. La Goulette, a coastal neighbourhood of Tunis with bobbing fishing boats and a lively café culture, was developed and built up by Italian immigrants, who made up half of the community right up until the 1950s. It makes sense, then, that this hearty chickpea (garbanzo) stew would remind me of the comforting soups I've enjoyed and loved off-season in Puglia.

Made exceptional with the addition of spicy harissa, cumin and turmeric, lablebi is a staple of Tunisian cuisine, though its origins can also belinked to the Ottoman occupation of Tunis in the 1600s, when chickpeas were served to Ottoman soldiers as a thrifty and filling meal. It's hot, it's hearty and it's one of my favourite dishes in this book. This is a dish designed to warm you from the inside out and is the perfect go-to recipe if you ever feel a cold coming on.

Beware that this recipe of Latifa's is for those well versed in spice. If you want a more mellow *lablebi*, halve or even quarter the harissa quantity and then add more at the end if you need it, along with the other toppings.

SERVES 4-6

INGREDIENTS

500 g (1 lb 2 oz/2¼ cups) dried chickpeas (garbanzos)

2 teaspoons bicarbonate of soda (baking soda)

2 litres (68 fl oz/8½ cups) water

70 ml (2¼ oz/⅓ cup) olive oil

½ bulb of garlic, cloves thinly sliced

½ teaspoon ground black pepper

2 teaspoons ground cumin

1 teaspoon ground turmeric

1 tablespoon harissa, plus extra to serve

½ tablespoon sea salt

4-6 slices of days-old bread

TO SERVE

capers

poached or boiled eggs

good-quality tinned tuna

1. The day before, put the chickpeas into a large bowl, add the half the bicarbonate of soda, cover with water and leave to soak overnight.

2. The next day, drain the chickpeas, then place in a large saucepan with the water. Place over a high heat and start to bring to the boil as you add the remaining bicarbonate of soda followed by the oil, garlic, pepper, cumin, turmeric and harissa. Cover, leaving almost completely (leaving a space uncovered for the steam to escape) and bring to the boil, then reduce the heat to a steady simmer and cook for 20 minutes.

3. After this time, add the salt, then simmer for a further 20 minutes. Check to see if the chickpeas have softened by taking a few out and pressing on them with a fork or, even better, tasting them, to make sure they are soft.

4. When you're ready to serve, break up the bread into the bottom of bowls and top up with the *lablebi* (you can choose to have it dense like a stew or loose like a ramen), then top with the other toppings as you like.

'I've been eating lablebi since I was a little girl. It's our 'fast food' here in Tunis – the thing young people eat at 5 o'clock in the morning after a night out in the city. In some regions of Tunisia they serve it inside a baguette, like a sandwich. It soaks up the alcohol after a heavy night. Of course, I wouldn't know about this because when I was a young girl I was mainly kept indoors. I grew up in the Medina, but I rarely saw it because I wasn't allowed to play outside. We were seven children in total and my brothers were the only ones of us that were allowed to venture out. I didn't know any different and this was the norm, so I never questioned it.'

LATIFA — B. 1945 — TUNIS — TUNISIA

Giovanna's Fave Nette con Cicoria Matta
Pugliese Fava with Wild Chicory

Giovanna is one of those nonnas I get along with instantly. She takes no warming up at all and, upon shaking my hand and ushering me into her 1970s-tiled kitchen, she says, 'You're definitely not what I was expecting today.' Much to my relief, she explains she was waiting for someone a lot older and more serious-looking to show up.

As she is from the Apulian countryside, Giovanna has chosen a dish that represents her region. This wholesome and hearty dish of puréed broad (fava) beans and wilted chicory doused in olive oil is common in Puglia. Broad beans have always been cheap and easy to cultivate and the bitter chicory leaf grows wild in the region and is foraged in the winter months.

This makes for a soothing midweek meal once the weather takes a turn towards the pallid but I have also tried it cold – with the addition of capers, thinly sliced red onion and sun-dried tomatoes – to great success in the summer months. You can also swap out the chicory for wilted beetroot (beet) tops, kale or even Tenderstem broccoli (broccolini) if that's what you have to hand. It's as versatile and easy to get along with as Giovanna herself. The only thing she insists on is enjoying it with a glass of wine or a beer.

SERVES 4–6

INGREDIENTS

500 g (1 lb 2 oz/2½ cups) dried broad (fava) beans, soaked overnight

100 ml (3½ fl oz/scant ½ cup) olive oil, plus extra to serve

1 garlic clove, peeled

1 kg (2 lb 4 oz) wild chicory leaves, washed well and roughly chopped

1 scant tablespoon salt, plus extra for the chicory

crusty bread, to serve

1. Put the soaked beans into a saucepan and cover with about 2.5 cm (1 inch) water. Cover and gently bring to the boil over a medium heat, then cook on a rolling boil for around five minutes until foam begins to cover the surface of the water. When this happens, scoop the foam off before reducing to a low simmer and cooking for 40–50 minutes, or until the beans are soft. Before the beans finish cooking, set aside a ladle or two of the cooking water in case you need to use it to loosen the purée later.

2. Meanwhile, sauté the chicory using half the olive oil in a non-stick frying pan, adding the garlic and a sprinkle of salt before putting the lid on. You want the leaves to be soft and wilted, with a little resistance if you stick a fork in them.

3. Once the beans have softened and most of the water has boiled off, use a hand-held blender to blend the beans to a purée, adding a dash of the remaining olive oil and the salt. If it becomes more of a paste than a purée and is too thick and stodgy, add a little of the reserved cooking water bit by bit until it loosens up again.

4. Plate and serve alongside the wilted chicory, with a heavy dousing of olive oil and a hefty wedge of crusty sourdough bread. Giovanna insists on drinking wine from Salento with hers, or else at least a beer.

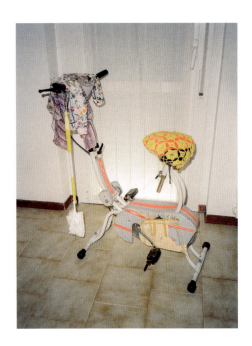

'We ate fave a lot when I was growing up and it's still very much in my repertoire. One day it would be fave, the next day chickpeas (garbanzos), another day green beans. We grew up on vegetables mainly and if we ate pasta, it would be on a Sunday with cime di rapa, not every day of the week. Pasta was a special plate rather than commonplace most days of the week and meat was also once a week, if that.

I couldn't tell you how many plates of fave this red pan of mine has cooked up. I've had it for 60 years and it's still good as new. My mother used an old wooden spoon to purée the beans. I'm still very impressed by that because, of course, I've become accustomed to using the hand blender. She would just bash, bash, bash away with the wooden spoon, working up a sweat over the stove to make sure it was a nice, smooth consistency.

We call the chicory that goes with this dish matta (crazy) because it grows wild. I remember picking this in the cold winter months while snow was on the ground when I was just a little girl. Times were very different then and I stopped going to school when I was 10 years old. I would work the land with my family: from sunrise to sunset we were out in those olive groves picking olives in the rain, or else sowing and harvesting vegetables. That's what it was like growing up in the south. We relied on our own hands and the strength of our bodies to get us through the day and for the land to provide enough to ensure every mouth was fed.

Not many people went to school back in those days and I suppose I was lucky to have received some sort of an education. Between the ages of 10 and 12 I worked out on the land with my parents and helped with jobs at home. It wasn't until the age of 12 that I was actually paid for a day of labour, though. Two entire years of work with no pay. Now it's hard to find young people to work the land. They don't want to do that kind of work and yet the kind of jobs they want don't exist in the south so they either move to cities or they live off their parents' income. The fields I toiled in as a girl have been abandoned. Like this, slowly, slowly, we're becoming disconnected from the land.'

GIOVANNA — B. 1940 — PUGLIA — ITALY

Italia's Patate Arraganate
Napolese Oregano Baked Potatoes

Nonna Italia is the first Italian grandmother I cooked with for this book, and I can't think of a more Italian experience than the welcome I received to her home in Pozzuoli, the hometown of Sophia Loren, which is a 20-minute drive along the coast from Naples.

When I arrive, she kisses me on either cheek and – together with five other Neapolitans – insists that I can't have a glass of water but must drink wine. 'Water isn't good for the bones, you'll rust,' they tell me. Apparently this is something you'll hear often in Naples. I am straight off a flight from Athens and completely parched but I roll with it.

I tell Italia that I love her name. With an eye roll and a dismissive wave of her veined hand, she explains that her father was a fascist: 'There were many Italias, Italios, Benitas and Benitos in those days.'

In her small kitchen, warm afternoon light spilling through embroidered curtains onto a mishmash of patterns, Italia shows me how to make this roasted potato *contorno* (side dish), which she usually makes with roast lamb at Easter. There's an absolute cacophony the entire time as other family members pop in and out to top up our wine or comment on the cooking process. I am nipped at by her very protective dog, Teddy, on more than one occasion and then force-fed sausage and *friarielli* (rapini) during the cooking process, in spite of my protests. Then of course, more wine.

It's complete sensory overload and I think, 'Welcome to Italia.' The feeling of warmth and the sense of being a part of a family within minutes is something I've only experienced in southern Europe. It's chaos but I adore it.

This dish is from the Cilento region – a part of Magna Grecia, as it is known to the Italians – and Italia says all the flavours in this aromatic dish come from Greece. It's true that I haven't seen oregano used very much in Italian cooking but it's definitely a staple in Greek cuisine. We use dried oregano from the mountains, foraged by Italia's son, along with generous glugs of olive oil. The result is gloriously golden potatoes with a crispy texture thanks to the addition of breadcrumbs and two different types of cheese. Don't be tempted to skimp on the olive oil – this is where all the flavour and that golden tone come from.

INGREDIENTS

50 ml (1 3/4 fl oz/3½ tablespoons) olive oil

1 kg (2 lb 4 oz) floury potatoes, peeled and chopped into small 1.5 cm (½ inch) cubes

1 bunch of parsley, leaves roughly chopped

150 g (5½ oz/generous 1¾ cups) fresh breadcrumbs

4 garlic cloves, finely chopped

3 tablespoons dried oregano

½ teaspoon freshly ground black pepper

1 teaspoon salt

20 g (¾ oz) pecorino, grated

20 g (¾ oz) Parmesan, grated

1. Preheat the oven to 170°C fan (375°F).
2. Pour the oil into a medium-sized baking tray (pan) or casserole dish (Dutch oven), then add the potatoes, shaking them to coat them in the oil. Follow with the rest of the ingredients, turning the potatoes over and over to ensure they ingredients are all evenly dispersed.
3. Bake in the oven for 40–50 minutes, or until the potatoes are golden brown.

'When I make this dish, I have my mother in mind, because she was the one who taught me to cook. She was a beautiful mamma and an incredible cook. Patate arraganate is a dish for the poor, because we were a huge family with so many mouths to feed, but it's tasty and the scent of the oregano transports me back in time to my mother's kitchen. I was one of 10 siblings and now I am the only one left of all of them. I have such an intense nostalgia for the past. It's such a sweet sorrow I feel when I think of my mother and my sisters. I loved them all so much.

    I have lived a long life and I have outlived all of my siblings, despite half of them being younger than me. If there's any bit of advice I can give from my years on this earth it's to not hold onto material things. Don't lust after things. Things won't satisfy you. They will just make you long and yearn and strive for something you will never feel that you're attaining. If you have less, you have less to lose.'

ITALIA — B. 1935 — CILENTO — ITALY

Maria Addolorata's Orecchiette con Cime di Rapa
Pugliese Pasta with Cime di Rapa

In the very far north of Puglia, Maria Addolorata ('Maria the sorrowful', named after the patron saint of her town) lives surrounded by lush green fields and the Apulian mountains. Locals call this the Tavoliere, which is the name this nonna also gives to the large wooden board that she uses to roll her orecchiette on. Apricena was once a mining region, but now the industry has trickled out. San Severo, known to be the headquarters of the local mafia, is the neighbouring town, and the area is steeped in poverty.

Still, we eat a plentiful lunch of fresh mozzarella in hefty, chewy white balls and tomatoes that sing with the flavours of summer in the company of Maria Addolorata and her granddaughters. As she welcomes me into her kitchen, she says her house is 'small'. I say it's abundant in everything you can hope for in life: good-quality fresh ingredients, family and love. Plus, an impressive collection of original 1960s furnishings and the kinds of tiles that I can spend all day photographing.

There can be nothing more satisfying than eating your own homemade pasta and I find this, of all the shapes, to be one of the easiest and most satisfying to master. Orecchiette (meaning 'little ears' on account of their shape) with cime di rapa (rapini) is a pasta dish that is surprisingly light. The cime di rapa – a loose relation to broccoli but with a finer stem – is cooked until very soft, so that it breaks down into a sauce around the homemade pasta. As an alternative to cime di rapa, you can use broccoli and its leaves or Tenderstem broccoli (broccolini). The key here is to add a good drizzle of quality olive oil at the end.

SERVES 2

INGREDIENTS

220 g (7¾ oz/1¾ cups) fine durum wheat flour (semola rimacinata/semolina/farina), or as needed

½ tablespoon extra virgin olive oil, plus extra to serve

100 ml (3½ fl oz/scant ½ cup) lukewarm water, or as needed

100 g (3½ oz) cime di rapa (rapini), trimmed (or Tenderstem broccoli/broccolini)

flaky sea salt

1. Tip 180 g (6½ oz/scant 1½ cups) of the flour onto a clean work surface and make a well in the centre. Pour the oil into the well and add a pinch of salt.

2. Add a little of the water to the well (go slowly, as you may not need the full amount, depending on your flour) and start to work the flour into the water at the edges of the well using your fingers in a circular motion, pulling in enough to absorb the water. Repeat until all the flour is incorporated and a dough starts to form – it should be fairly scraggy at this point but you can use your hands to scrunch the dough together into a more cohesive lump.

3. Now start to knead the dough – it shouldn't be dry or sticky, so if it is, add a touch more water or flour accordingly. Knead for 10–15 minutes, using the heel of your palms to push the dough away from you and your fingers to pull it back and fold it over, turning the dough clockwise as you go – this will make it soft, smooth and slightly bouncy.

4. Once the dough is in a smooth ball, cover it with a damp dish cloth or cling film (plastic wrap) and leave to sit for 10 minutes at room temperature.

5. Once rested, break off a small section of the dough and roll it out into a long, 1 cm (½ inch) thick rope-like shape with the palms of your hands against the work surface. Make sure to re-cover the rest of the dough so it doesn't dry out while you work.

6. Using a sharp knife, cut the rope into small pillows, about 1 cm (½ inch) long. These will become your orecchiette. Find a blunt knife with a rounded tip and sprinkle a little of the remaining flour on the work surface. Hold the knife so that the blade faces away from you (almost flat) and press the edge of the tip lightly but firmly into one of the pillows of dough at the edge farthest from you, at a slight angle. Drag it along the surface towards you, applying consistent pressure. It should curl over the knife. Flick the piece of dough off the knife and turn it inside out by pushing your thumb into the crevice to help create a dome shape. The dome should have a slightly rough texture, which will help to hold on to flavour when cooked.

7. Get a rhythm going to shape the rest of the orecchiette in the same way, placing them on a baking sheet lined with baking parchment or a board to dry out a little while you repeat the process with the rest of the dough.

8. Bring a saucepan of water to the boil and add 1 tablespoon salt. Add the cime di rapa and simmer for 5 minutes, or until nice and tender. Remove with a slotted spoon and set aside in a bowl.

9. Add the pasta to the same water and cook for 2–4 minutes over a medium-high heat until al dente. Add the cime di rapa back in for a second to reheat, then drain all together.

10. Serve and add a drizzle of olive oil before tucking in.

'Patience and time are needed to make a good meal and, inevitably, having patience helps in life. This orecchiette is not like the one you will find in Bari. It's the original orecchiette that takes time to shape and needs a little more patience than just flipping out a shape quickly with the tip of your knife. What I mean by this is that the pieces of dough I use are much smaller and the technique used to shape it requires an extra flick of the fingers to ensure a daintier piece of pasta. What they make in Bari looks like the skullcap of a priest, that's not orecchiette.

Patience and time help to heal what life has to throw at you. My daughter died when she was just 20 years old. She had a problem with her heart and from one moment to the next, we lost her. It was so unexpected and I suffered terribly. I still do. The pain doesn't pass, but what helped me at the time was my husband. He was a beautiful man – I met him aged 16. When this happened to us, we cried together, we held each other. When I was weak, he supported me, and vice versa.

This taught me how important it is to find a good partner to accompany you through life.

When I met my husband, I didn't care if he worked or what kind of job he did. I just felt he was the right man for me. He looked like an actor. Together, we were the most beautiful couple.

You can tell right from the start if this person will be the one for you. It's something you will feel deep down and if you realise it isn't working out further down the line, you'll probably know that this feeling was there with you from the start, surfacing from deep inside you to warn that this was not your path all along.'

MARIA ADDOLORATA — B. 1932 — APRICENA — ITALY

Chiara's Spaghetti all'Amatriciana

Chiara, my mother-in-law, saves my life every time we visit her at home in Italy, where she splits her time between a stylish apartment in the heart of Milan and a leafy lakeside paradise on Lago Maggiore. She entertains Calypso for hours and manages to cook for the entire family at the same time.

What amazes me most is that she seems able to whip up a tasty three-course meal at a moment's notice. Perhaps it's the Italian nonnas' way. Despite Chiara's aversion to all things green, I still love what she puts on the table. She cooks the way she dresses: with flare, confidence and ease.

Over the many years that she worked as a fashion stylist in Milan, she needed a go-to dinner for the family that came together with little fuss and effort but yielded maximum results. This spaghetti all'Amatriciana is an easy one that she learned to rustle up quickly.

Chiara insists that you always use guanciale and never EVER break the spaghetti into the pan of boiling water. Her preferred pasta brand is Rummo, but she says, in all seriousness, 'Anything is better than Barilla.'

SERVES 4

INGREDIENTS

1 heaped tablespoon coarse sea salt

1 tablespoon olive oil

1 small red onion, finely chopped

100 g (3½ oz) guanciale, chopped into 5 mm (¼ inch) cubes

1 dried red chilli (or ½ teaspoon chilli (hot pepper) flakes)

1 x 400 g (14 oz) tin of chopped tomatoes

½ teaspoon caster (superfine) sugar

pinch of sea salt

400 g (14 oz) spaghetti

4 tablespoons grated pecorino

1. Pour 2.5 litres (84½ fl oz/10½ cups) water into a large saucepan, add the coarse sea salt and leave to come to the boil while you start the sauce.

2. Heat the oil in a non-stick frying pan over a medium heat and fry the onion for a few minutes until soft, then add the guanciale and continue to sizzle for up to five minutes until it browns, stirring often.

3. Now add the dried chilli – you can leave it whole or chop it up with the seeds (the seeds will make it spicier, so be warned!) – and stir in. Next, add the chopped tomatoes, followed by the sugar and a pinch of salt. Leave the sauce to simmer away over a low-medium flame while you cook the spaghetti.

4. Add the spaghetti to the boiling water and cook exactly to the recommended time on the packet (Nonna Chiara checks hers by tasting it periodically).

5. Once the sauce has thickened, remove it from the heat. Drain the pasta and transfer it back to the saucepan along with the sauce. Add the grated pecorino and mix well to combine.

'I don't come from a great line of cooking nonnas. The nonnas in my family haven't been particularly present, in all honesty. My paternal grandmother was the one I knew, because the other died when I was still young. She came from a very Catholic family, so she had 13 children, which meant she was incredibly stretched for time. I remember that she was very beautiful, but she didn't have a lot of time for me because she was very preoccupied with the entire family and had to spread herself very thin.

My own mother definitely never cooked for me or took care of my children, very much defying the stereotype of the classic Italian nonna. She was never really a mother to me or my siblings. Of course, I worked when I had my children, and I had a life beyond raising my family, but my mother never worked. She was just preoccupied with travelling and doing her own thing rather than being there for us. She didn't accompany me to school once. Not even on the first day. To counterbalance her failings, I had a great relationship with my father and I am very grateful to have been gifted such a compassionate and generous father figure in life. I never wanted to be like my mother, who hasn't been a particularly present grandmother. I want my grandchildren to know me and I love spending time with them.'

CHIARA — B. 1955 — MILAN — ITALY

Anna's Polpette di Ricotta
Pugliese Ricotta Balls in Tomato Sauce

Nonna Anna lives in a small village just outside of Lecce. The pastel-toned single-storey houses look more akin to those of a Spanish colonial town than the limestone facades of Lecce and I comment on this while we make her famous *polpette di ricotta*, a great vegetarian alternative to the ubiquitous Italian meatballs in 'red sauce'. She uses fresh sheep's milk ricotta for hers, nodding to the abundance of sheep's cheeses in the Apulian region of Italy.

Anna knows her history. She comes alive explaining that southern Italy has taken influence from its neighbouring countries and the colonial powers that once settled here. We exchange notes on Greek and Italian Easter traditions and I realise that my village's annual hike into the hills of south Corfu on Easter Monday also happens in the Salento region. '*Una faccia una razza*,' (one face, one race) says Nonna Anna and squeezes my cheek. Corfu can be seen from the southernmost tip of Puglia, so our proximity has meant an obvious interchange of influences. Both in Salento and on my island, people take to nature to enjoy a picnic on Easter Monday, even eating a sweet bread with a boiled egg baked into it.

This dish is an easy midweek vegetarian meal that is both filling and full of flavour. Serve simply with crusty bread and a generous glass of Primitivo. Anna emphasises the importance of using good-quality passata and ricotta.

SERVES 4–6

INGREDIENTS

500 g (1 lb 2 oz) ricotta

100 g (3½ oz) pecorino, grated (or another Italian hard cheese)

175 g (6 oz/¾ cup) dried breadcrumbs

handful of parsley, leaves finely chopped

1 large egg, beaten

salt and freshly ground black pepper

FOR THE SAUCE

3 tablespoons olive oil

1 small white onion, halved

500 g (1 lb 2 oz/ 2 cups) passata (sieved tomatoes)

750 ml (25 fl oz/ 3 cups) water

small bunch of basil, stems and all (set aside a few leaves to serve)

2 teaspoons coarse salt

1. Drain any excess liquid from the ricotta, then spoon it into a large bowl with all the other ingredients for the polpette. Season with salt and pepper and mix until well combined, using your hands at the end to really bring everything together in a squishing motion. It should be easy to handle; soft enough to roll into a ball and firm enough to hold its shape. If it's too sticky, you can add more breadcrumbs, or if it's too dry, add water, a teaspoon at a time.

2. Working quickly, start rolling and shaping the mixture into walnut-sized balls in your hands (around 30 g/1 oz each) and place on a tray lined with baking parchment. The mixture should make around 25 balls. Set aside in the refrigerator while you make the sauce.

3. Place a large, wide saucepan or sauté pan (about 28 cm/11 inches in diameter) over a medium-high heat and add all the ingredients for the sauce. Cover and bring to the boil, then reduce to a simmer and cook for 15 minutes, removing the lid for the final 5 minutes. You want it to reduce and thicken a little but still be quite saucy.

4. Carefully remove the onion and basil and season to taste. Place the polpette in the sauce, in a single layer across the bottom, if possible. Use a spoon to make sure they are covered with the sauce, then cover and cook over a medium heat for 8–10 minutes, or until they are tender and cooked through.

5. Serve in shallow bowls with plenty of sauce, topped with extra basil.

'In Pugliese dialect, polpette are known as cocule, meaning to 'ball up'. This is a dish that we make here in Salento in the days leading up to Easter. Traditionally, polpette are made with minced (ground) meat, but we don't eat meat during Lent so this is a great vegetarian alternative. I remember making this with my own nonna and great-grandmother, too. It's a recipe that has been passed down through so many generations and I feel privileged to share it. I can't believe that some people are so secretive about sharing their recipes. It's not like we can cook from the comfort of our graves, is it?

When I hear people speaking puritanically about the food here in Italy it makes me laugh. Without experimentation and the changing of recipes and mixing of cultural influences, the food that we eat wouldn't be as rich as it is today. In the south of Italy, we've been colonised by so many different ruling powers. The Spanish came, the Greeks came, the Arabs came. The Mediterranean facilitated this great blending of flavours we have in our food, so when I hear someone saying 'Oh no, this recipe should only be made in this way,' I have to laugh. The same goes to the sentiment against immigrants. I can't understand why you would want to stop this great exchange of cultures.

Everything in our culinary culture has a purpose and I find it fascinating. For example, in the north of Italy, pasta is made with egg. Here in the south, our grains have a lot of protein, so we never had the necessity to add egg to our pasta dough.

The same goes for religion and the rituals it has left us with. We eat fish on a Friday and meat on a Sunday. These were the 'rules' laid down by the Catholic Church but this also meant that we lived a more balanced lifestyle. Everything had a sort of logic to it, even if it masqueraded as religion. After breaking our 40 days of Lent and feasting on Easter Sunday, we then picnic on Easter Monday, eating lighter foods to make up for all of the gluttony of the day before.

As a girl, I would go and picnic in the olive grove with my family on Easter Monday, pasquetta. We would take these polpette di ricotta along with a few other things to snack on. Everyone picnics on Easter Monday. It's a tradition we've held on to for centuries. I remember we'd head to a small shelter in the woods that was built by labourers so that they could hide from the rain, and we'd picnic near there. This dish always reminds me of those spring days with my family.'

ANNA — B. 1947 — PUGLIA — ITALY

Alfia's Parmigiana di Melanzane
One Pan Sicilian Aubergine Parmigiana

Alfia lives on the west coast of Sicily in the seaside town of Riposto. The streets here are washed in different tones of pastel and the houses, on first glance, appear to be small – but after I step into Alfia's home, I realise that the humble exterior of the building has fooled me. Each room opens up into another space, the kitchen being the last, with Alfia framed in its doorway at the end of a seemingly never-ending corridor of rooms.

Each space has its own unique feel. The fancy dining room flooded with light is the first room that people encounter when stepping in off the street. I sense it is the least lived in. People walking by can steal a glance and spot a smart, marble-topped mid-century dining table with elegant chairs (the seats still wrapped in plastic), a decadent hanging lamp, a 1950s radio tucked into the corner, covered with framed family photographs, and a decadent vitrine with Alfia's best crockery and glassware. Next is Alfia's bedroom, the dimmest room in the house (by design!), with her impeccably made marital bed at its centre, rosary hanging above it. Following that is a wood-panelled room that opens up into a sun-drenched courtyard that meets the kitchen, where Alfia spends most of her time.

Alfia's home is characterful in every way and filled with beautiful antique furniture as well as the customary hand-knitted throws, net curtains and icons of the Madonna tucked into corners full of knick-knacks. She is an open-hearted lady who is cheerful and welcoming from the very start. The parmigiana di melanzane she makes tastes delicious. When these three elements come together, we have the makings of a satisfying day of cooking and shooting together.

I'm intensely moved when Alfia begins to cry, lamenting the years of life that have passed her by. I am in an intense moment of life myself, having just become a mother and struggling with my new identity. Meeting Alfia makes me even more determined to hold onto the woman I was before bringing Calypso into this world. I so want to live my life, filled with passion and colour in every moment. Alfia made the ultimate sacrifice for her family, but she did it at a time in which that was her only choice. Our conversation makes me think about how I want to look back on my own life when I'm her age.

Indulgent layers of crispy breadcrumbs, sticky aubergine (eggplant), mozzarella and sweet passata make this parmigiana a source of comfort. Cook this when your life and everything in it is in question. I'm not saying it will solve anything, but it certainly will keep you occupied and nourished. Don't expect to assemble it in a tray and simply stick it in the oven, though. In Nonna Alfia's words, 'A real parmigiana di melanzane is not baked in an oven.' This is a fun one to make and requires a little courage. You'll need to flip a frying pan in order to get a crispy finish on both sides of the parmigiana. Alfia flips the whole thing like a pro no less than four times to ensure a nicely toasted outer breadcrumb layer.

SERVES 6

INGREDIENTS

700 ml (24 fl oz/scant 3 cups) sunflower oil

1 kg (2 lb 4 oz) aubergines (eggplants), sliced into 1 cm (½ inch) rounds

3 medium eggs

90 g (3¼ oz) dried breadcrumbs

10 g (½ oz) Parmesan, grated

200 g (7 oz) mozzarella, sliced

FOR THE SAUCE

400 g (14 oz/generous ¾ cup) passata (sieved tomatoes)

60 ml (2 fl oz/¼ cup) water

1 teaspoon granulated sugar

1 tablespoon salt

handful of basil leaves, plus extra to serve (optional)

2 garlic cloves, finely chopped or grated

1. Heat the oil in a large frying pan (about 32 cm/12½ inches wide) over a medium heat and fry the aubergines in batches for up to five minutes or until nice and soft and golden. Place the fried aubergine slices on a tray lined with paper towels to soak up the excess oil.

2. Meanwhile get your eggs and sauce ready. Bring a saucepan of water to the boil and cook the eggs for 10 minutes, then plunge them into cold water and allow to cool before peeling and chopping them.

3. Combine all the ingredients for the sauce in a saucepan over a medium heat and simmer for 10 minutes, or until reduced and thickened.

4. Once all the aubergines are fried, pour out all but a little bit of oil from the frying pan, then sprinkle half the breadcrumbs and half the Parmesan over the base of the pan. Add an even layer of aubergines (placed snugly side by side, not overlapping), a layer of chopped egg and some mozzarella. Next, spoon over some of the sauce – you want it to be nicely coated rather than drowning in sauce as you will have to flip this later, so use around 150 g (5½ oz). We are aiming for three layers of aubergine, but if your pan is larger, go for two layers and use a bit less sauce.

5. Working quickly, so the bottom layer of breadcrumbs doesn't get soggy, repeat with another layer of aubergine, egg, mozzarella and sauce. Finish with a final layer of aubergines, and the remaining Parmesan and breadcrumbs on top. Place the pan over a medium-high heat and fry for 3–5 minutes, allowing the breadcrumbs on the bottom to crust and the mixture to heat through.

6. Now remove the pan from the heat and carefully place a large plate over the top of the frying pan. With oven gloves on, hold the plate in place and flip the pan over so that the parmigiana falls onto the plate. Remove the frying pan from the top (hopefully to reveal a nice golden crust!), put it back on the heat for 30 seconds and slide the parmigiana gently back into the pan from the plate. Fry for a further 3–5 minutes until the breadcrumbs on the bottom are golden and have formed a crust. To serve, flip one more time onto a serving plate and take to the table. Top with a few fresh basil leaves, if liked.

'I never had a youth, and it makes me sad to think about the years that were lost to hard work here in this house. I was sent to work as a child. From the age of around 12, I helped a noble family with housework, odd chores and errands. It was in this role that I learned to cook. A lady called Giovannina, who also worked for the family, passed on her knowledge to me and it's her I have to thank for all that I learned in the kitchen. She was a brilliant cook, and I still don't think I've learned to conjure the magic that she did, even after all these years. This parmigiana recipe comes from her, and I make it in the exact same way that I learned to make it as a girl. Other people do it in the oven but in the pan is the only real way you should make a parmigiana.

I don't have regrets, but I do think about the years that have passed with a sense of sadness because I married very young. My husband was a good man, but he didn't open up and I was a girl that needed words. I wanted someone to tell me that I was beautiful and that they loved me, but this never came from him and I suffered because of it. We just didn't speak the same language when it came to love.

I think, in many ways, things have become so much better for women since I was younger but this should have changed a long time ago. That way, I might have had a better time as a young girl. I was expected to work all morning at the house upstairs, cleaning and cooking for another family, and then I would return home and my husband would want lunch to be ready and waiting for him on the table. This was a man who was much better than the husbands my friends had. At least he gave me an element of freedom. If I had married another man, it may have been three times worse. Still, I wish we could have done more things together, taken trips or gone out more. Or that he'd been more affectionate. The years have passed now and my chances for that kind of romance have gone with them.'

ALFIA — B. 1939 — RIPOSTO — ITALY

Carmela's Pasta alla Norma
Sicilian Aubergine Tortiglioni

Nonna Carmela is taking a break from her 12-bedroom house in the Sicilian countryside to live with her daughter in the city of Catania for a few months. Luckily for me, the dates she's in town match up with my inbound flight to Catania, so she's the nonna that welcomes me back to my beloved Sicily after a four-year hiatus.

In true Sicilian style, she has decided on pasta alla Norma as our 'primo'.

This pasta dish sings of the flavours of a Mediterranean summer. Rich tomato passata, fragrant basil and sweet aubergine (eggplant) slick with olive oil make for the perfect midweek meal. It also tastes delicious cold and can be made in advance and eaten as a pasta salad at a garden party or as part of a picnic. Carmela followed this up with the best tiramisu of my life.

SERVES 4

INGREDIENTS

2 small aubergines (eggplants), two thirds cut into 1 cm (½ inch) slices and one third chopped into 2 cm (¾ inch) cubes

1 teaspoon sea salt, plus extra to taste

150 ml (5 fl oz/scant ⅔ cup) extra virgin olive oil

1 small onion, thinly sliced into half-moons

250 g (9 oz/1 cup) passata rustica (chunky sieved tomatoes)

150 ml (5 fl oz/scant ⅔ cup) water

5 basil leaves, roughly torn

400 g (14 oz) tortiglioni

freshly ground black pepper

ricotta salata or Parmesan, grated, to serve

1. Prepare the aubergines by placing the pieces in a bowl and sprinkling with the salt. Set aside for at least 10 minutes, then rinse under cool water and set aside. You can skip this step if you like, but it does make the aubergines extra tasty.

2. Heat 100 ml (3½ fl oz/scant ½ cup) of the oil in a large, non-stick frying pan over a medium heat, then fry the aubergines in batches for around 5 minutes until golden brown all over (but not too crispy). Remove with a slotted spoon and place on a plate lined with paper towels to soak up any extra grease.

3. Heat the remaining oil in a saucepan over a medium-low heat, then gently cook the onion for 10–15 minutes until nice and soft and beginning to turn golden, but not get crispy.

4. Add the passata and water to the onions (use the water to rinse out the passata bottle like Carmela does) and bring to the boil. Reduce to a simmer, then add the basil and leave to bubble, uncovered, for 15–20 minutes until slightly reduced and thickened. Season to taste with salt and black pepper.

5. Meanwhile, bring a large saucepan of water to the boil and cook the pasta until al dente, according to the packet instructions. Once it's ready, drain the pasta and add it to your saucepan, stirring to combine it with the aubergine and *sugo*, then transfer it back to the pan. Divide between plates and sprinkle with ricotta salata or Parmesan to serve.

'Pasta alla Norma is eaten all over Sicily and is rich in all the produce that we grow here on the island. The aubergine is something you'll find again and again in many of our dishes, but I like it with pasta.

I always use my own passata and I wouldn't have it any other way. When the tomatoes are nice and ripe, I wake up at 1 a.m. to begin the process of making my passata. It takes a good 10 hours of work to work with 60 kg [132 lb] of tomatoes and all the bottles and jars you need to sterilise to store the passata. I have to wash them, remove all the skins and then simmer them in huge vats to have passata that will last me throughout the winter. It really is something though, when you're finished and you go down to the pantry and see all the jars and bottles of your own passata lined up. It's 10 hours of labour for an entire year of eating. Nothing tastes as good as your own hard work.'

CARMELA — B. 1940 — MESSINA — ITALY

Am Samir's Syrian Oozy Filo Rice Parcels

DEDICATION BY CHEF IMAD ALARNAB
This is a very nostalgic recipe from my childhood growing up in Syria, when I used to help my grandmother – or Am Samir, as we called her – to prepare these parcels for my family. Since I was very young, Am Samir always made these filo parcels by hand, carefully wrapping the rice mixture in pastry before handing them over to me to coat with melted ghee before they were baked in the oven.

My favourite part was smelling the burning ghee in the oven and then tucking into the first one, hot and fresh in my hand. The combination of the filo pastry and ghee gives them a satisfying crisp texture. It's such a sensory dish – just touching, smelling, looking or tasting these brings the warm memory of Am Samir to my mind.

MAKES 6 PARCELS

INGREDIENTS

450 g (1 lb) diced lamb leg

2 bay leaves

3 cardamom pods

2 cloves

200 g (7 oz/1 cup) long-grain rice

1 teaspoon cumin seeds

2 tablespoons olive oil

pinch of salt

½ teaspoon ground cardamom

½ teaspoon ground ginger

1 teaspoon baharat spice mix

200 g (7 oz/1⅓ cups) frozen peas

40 g (1½ oz) pine nuts, toasted

40 g (1½ oz) cashews, toasted and roughly chopped

½ teaspoon ground black pepper

270 g (9½ oz) ready-made filo pastry

4 tablespoons melted ghee

cucumber and yoghurt sauce, to serve

1. Put the lamb into a large saucepan and pour over enough water to cover (about 1 litre/34 fl oz/4¼ cups) and bring to the boil over a high heat. Once it starts to boil, skim off the foam that rises to the top with a spoon. Add the bay leaves, cardamom pods and cloves and reduce to a simmer. Cover and cook for 45–60 minutes until the lamb is soft. Strain the lamb, reserving the cooking water.

2. Meanwhile, wash the rice until the water runs clear, then soak in a bowl of cold water for 30 minutes, then drain again.

3. Toast the cumin seeds in the olive oil in a saucepan over a medium-high heat for a minute, then add the drained rice, salt and ground spices to the pan and cover half with reserved lamb cooking water and half fresh water – the liquid should come about 1 cm (½ inch) above the rice. Cover, increase the heat and bring to the boil, then immediately reduce to a very low simmer and cook for 15 minutes. Remove the pan from the heat and leave for 5 minutes. Fluff up the rice with a fork, then transfer to a tray to cool evenly.

4. Once everything had cooled, mix the lamb, rice, peas, nuts and black pepper together. Set aside.

5. Unroll the filo pastry and cover it with a dish towel (this is important as you don't want the pastry to dry out).

6. Preheat the oven to 180°C fan (400°F). Grease a shallow baking tray (pan) with some of the melted ghee.

7. Take one sheet of filo pastry and fold it in half and then in half again, so you have four layers. Press the pastry into a ramekin so that it moulds into the shape, but make sure you have enough overhang to be able to fold over the top later. Fill the pastry with the rice and lamb mixture, then fold the pastry over the mixture to close it up.

8. Working quickly, put a hand over the closed pastry and ramekin and flip it over onto the prepared tray, so you have an upside-down parcel. Brush generously with ghee and repeat with the remaining rice and pastry to make five more.

9. Bake in the oven for 30–35 minutes until the pastry is golden all over.

10. Serve with a cucumber and whipped yogurt sauce.

Perihan's Manti
Turkish Yoghurt Laced Lamb Dumplings

Perihan – or 'Pero' – is the grandmother of my good friend Sanem so when I meet her, I instantly feel at home in her embrace. She has the same impish smile that Sanem has, something cheeky going on behind the eyes that makes you warm to her. She lives in the heart of Izmir in a swelteringly hot apartment block and, of course, we've chosen the hottest day of the year so far to make *manti* – a dish usually reserved for cooler weather. We squeeze into her tiny kitchen and, not before long, Perihan is force-feeding both me and photographer Marco. I mean this in the very literal sense: she picks up our spoons, scoops up four *manti* in one go and shovels them into our mouths. More fool us for grabbing a *köfte* lunch before our visit.

These lamb-filled dumplings (aka pockets of grandmotherly love) coated in yoghurt are typical of Central Asia, the Caucasus and the Balkans, but they've made their way to the Mediterranean via women like Perihan, who have travelled with their recipes. The first time I tried them was in Athens and I've been obsessed with the feeling of comfort that a bowl of good *manti* can inspire ever since.

I find folding these much easier than rolling/shaping pasta and would go as far as saying the repetitive action can become quite meditative. It's a task that can also be fun to do with a friend. Traditionally, women would gather together to make *manti* and, inevitably, have a good gossip.

Perihan didn't do this, but I like to add a little dousing of chilli oil on top of the yoghurt, just for an extra kick.

SERVES 4

INGREDIENTS

FOR THE DOUGH

275 g (9¾ oz/scant 2¼ cups) plain (all-purpose) flour, plus extra for dusting

1 teaspoon salt

1 large egg

80 ml (2¾ fl oz/⅓ cup) water

FOR THE FILLING

250 g (9 oz) minced (ground) lamb

1 small onion, very finely diced or grated

10 g (½ oz) parsley, leaves finely chopped

1 teaspoon salt

⅓ teaspoon freshly ground black pepper

FOR THE YOGHURT SAUCE

500 g (1 lb 2 oz/2 cups) plain yoghurt

1–2 garlic cloves, finely chopped or grated (to taste)

½ tsp dried mint

sprinkle of sumac, chilli (hot pepper) flakes or chilli oil (optional)

1. First, make the dough. Combine the flour and salt in a large bowl, then make a well in the centre and crack in the egg. Beat the egg lightly with a fork and then incorporate the flour until it is all mixed in (it will be quite a dry and lumpy). Gradually add the water, using your hand to bring the dough together. You may not need all the water, so stop when your dough feels springy rather than sticky.

2. Dust a work surface with flour and knead the dough for up to 5 minutes but no longer. It will probably look a little dimpled to start, but when it is ready it will be smooth, a little firmer and more elastic. If your dough starts feeling sticky, work in a sprinkle more flour. Once you're happy with it, divide it into two pieces, place in a bowl, cover the bowl with a damp dish towel and leave it to rest for 30 minutes at room temperature.

3. Meanwhile, make the filling. Combine all the ingredients in a bowl and mix well, breaking up the meat and massaging everything together until it's fully combined – using your hands is best. Set aside.

4. Meanwhile, whip up your yoghurt sauce by whisking together the yoghurt, garlic and mint in a bowl. A top granny tip is to leave the yoghurt out of the refrigerator at this point, so that it's room temperature by the time you serve your *manti* – you don't want your cosy dumpling dish going cold right away.

5. Now return to the dough. Dust the surface with flour again and roll out the dough with a rolling pin to create a large and thin (2 mm/⅛ inch) circle from which you'll cut out your individual *manti*. Once rolled out, use your rolling pin as a guide to draw lines with a sharp knife down the dough so that the width of the pin becomes the width of your *manti*. Move across the dough, drawing vertical lines with your knife so that it becomes individual strips, then turn the rolling pin 90 degrees and do the same thing to create a sheet of squares. The measurements will vary slightly, but they should be roughly 5 x 5 cm (2 x 2 inch).

6. Take a ¼–½ teaspoon-sized amount of filling and dot it into the middle of each square. You should be able to judge by eye how much filling your dough can stretch around, but you could always jump to the next step to test one before continuing.

7. Once you've added the filling, fill a small bowl with water and place it next to you – this will be helpful for dabbing on the corners of the dough if it doesn't stick easily. Now begin to shape your parcels. Perihan does this by pulling the two diagonally opposite corners of the dough together over the meat and pinching them together in the centre. She then does the same with the other two corners, pinching everything together in the centre to envelope the meat. This will create a star or flower shape on top of the parcel.

8. Place the shaped *manti* onto a large floured tray as you make them. Repeat with the second ball of dough. If you have leftover filling, you can make lamb *köfte* for another occasion.

9. Once all the parcels are made, bring a large saucepan of salted water to the boil and cook the *manti* for 8–10 minutes.

10. Once the *manti* are ready, drain them and serve piping hot topped with the yoghurt sauce and a sprinkling of sumac or chilli flakes or a drizzle of chilli oil.

'Manti isn't native to Izmir, where I live now. It is a recipe I've brought with me to the coast from Kars, a region that borders Syria and Russia. It's freezing cold up there in the north and not many vegetables grow. We made use of what was around, so meat and yoghurt were staples when I was growing up. Manti is a very warming dish. My mother taught me how to make this and it's a recipe I've kept close to me because of her and the frequency with which it appeared on the table in my childhood. She was a marvellous cook and I'm not just saying this because she was my mother. She and my grandmother were actually selected to cook for Atatürk when he visited Kars because they were such good cooks.

It was far too cold for me to live out all my days there, so I moved to Izmir in my forties. My home city was far from rural, though. It was modern and brimming with cultured people when I was young, but things seem to be going backwards because of our current, less than savoury, president.

I see myself as very progressive, but I was still a housewife all my life. I love cooking and hosting people and dedicating my life to raising my four children and grandchildren was a great use of my days on this earth. To watch them grow up and become good human beings is a very satisfying feeling. All of them went to university. It's incredibly important to me that they are educated people. Good schooling improves society and that, in turn, improves quality of life for all members of society.

I'm not sure what's going to become of Turkey in the coming years. All that our founding father, Atatürk, worked to do for us is being undone. The worst thing about it all is that women's rights are diminishing in this country. Many are murdered by their partners or ex-partners and conviction rates are not high. It's becoming acceptable in society that women are second class citizens. Of course, when women are at a disadvantage, the economy also suffers. So poverty is sky rocketing and people aren't at all happy.

I'm a mother and a grandmother and have always been economically dependent on men for my survival – either my father or my husband. It makes me very upset to see the situation hasn't changed. I just want my granddaughters to go to college and have independence. If I were young now, I would go to school, have a career and delay marriage. I was only 20 when I married. I was naive enough to just want to be a bride.'

PERIHAN — B. 1939 — KARS — TURKEY

Yvette's Soupe au Pistou
Provençal Pesto Minestrone Soup

SERVES 6

INGREDIENTS

2 tablespoons olive oil

1 white onion, thinly sliced

1 leek, thinly sliced

1.5 litres (50 fl oz/6⅓ cups) water

1 tablespoon salt

1 teaspoon freshly ground black pepper

100 g (3½ oz) freshly podded borlotti (cranberry) beans (or dried beans, soaked overnight)

100 g (3½ oz) red kidney beans, soaked (you can use tinned if you can't find dried)

2 large carrots, peeled and chopped into 1 cm (½ inch) cubes

2 garlic cloves

60 g (2 oz) green beans, cut into 1 cm (½ inch) pieces

60 g (2 oz) long green beans, cut into 1 cm (½ inch) pieces

2 waxy potatoes, peeled and chopped into 1 cm (½ inch) cubes

1 courgette (zucchini), chopped into 1 cm (½ inch) cubes

45 g (1½ oz) coquillette (elbow) pasta (or another short shape)

sliced Gruyère, to serve (optional)

FOR THE PISTOU

2 garlic cloves, green germs removed

20 g (¾ oz) basil leaves (about 1 bunch)

1 ripe beef (beefsteak) tomato, peeled and deseeded

150 ml (5 fl oz/scant ⅔ cup) extra virgin olive oil

coarse sea salt

Braux is a tiny village with only 80 permanent residents, most of them a gaggle of grannies that make up Mamie Yvette's friendship group. The three-hour drive from Marseille to her home in Provence is scented with lavender, which colours the rolling meadows of the French countryside lilac. To get to Yvette we pass sunflower fields that reach to the horizon, bright yellow servants to the sun, all turned east for the first rays of the morning. It is impossibly cinematic, and I feel as though I'm in a classic French film, so of course I crank up Edith Piaf and enjoy the cliché.

There are many similarities between Provençal cuisine and that of Liguria, the neighbouring Italian region, as proven by the *soupe au pistou* that Yvette shares with me. Singing with garlic and abundant in fresh summer vegetables that any great Provençal *grandmère* will have to hand in her garden, this dish is elevated by its tangy basil pesto and the comforting inclusion of a handful of pasta. It's a summer minestrone, and while I'm not one for soup in summer, this is one I make an exception for.

Don't be tempted to skimp on the basil – Yvette plundered her basil plant for this soup and it was worth it. Same goes for garlic, the ingredient that makes this (along with an optional addition of Gruyère cheese at the end) undeniably and irresistibly French.

1. Heat the oil in a large saucepan over a medium heat and gently fry the onion and leek for a few minutes until starting to soften.

2. Pour in the water, salt and pepper and add the borlotti and red kidney beans if you're using dry beans that have been soaking since the night before. If not, hold off on the beans. Bring the water to the boil, then simmer for 10 minutes.

3. After 10 minutes, add the carrots, borlotti beans and garlic and bring to a rolling boil then cover, reduce the heat to low and simmer for 15 minutes.

4. Next, add the green and long green beans, cover again and simmer for a further 15 minutes before adding the potatoes and courgette. If you're looking a little low on water, add a splash of hot water at this stage. Simmer for a further 20 minutes, covered, then add the pasta and cook for a final 10 minutes (use 10 minutes as a guideline but if your pasta's cooking instructions are for less time, follow those. If you are making this to eat later, cook the pasta in the soup just before serving to avoid it going soft). If you're using tinned kidney beans, add those now.

5. To make the pistou, put the garlic, basil and a pinch of salt into a large pestle and mortar and grind them to a paste. Using coarse sea salt helps with friction. Yvette warns against taking the easy way out and putting this in a blender – 'It will end up like washing up liquid,' she tells me.

6. Once well combined, add the tomato and the oil and continue to crush and combine with the pestle and mortar until you have a silky green pesto.

7. When it's ready, serve the soup topped with the pistou and add a slice or two of Gruyère for extra Provençal indulgence.

'When I was a young girl, the pistou didn't feature because we didn't have access to basil. My village is 1,000 metres (3,300 feet) above sea level, so it wasn't until I moved to nearby Dignes-les-Bains that pesto started to feature in my cooking. There were many things that made life difficult when living in such a remote region of France in those days. The schools were so far away that I had no choice but to board. From the age of 11 I was sent to what we call a pension – a school that we boarded at – to train as a teacher. It was distressing for me as such a young girl because I missed my parents dearly and could only go home four times a year. I remember crying a lot at school. This soup was always a small consolation.'

YVETTE — B. 1943 — BRAUX — FRANCE

Maryse's Courgette Gratin from Camargue

Mamie Maryse hails from the Camargue in the South of France, a coastal region known for its great produce. Markets in quaint rural towns here are taken seriously, with stallholders competing for the best arrangements of cheeses (the best I've seen was a pyramid of goat's cheese I didn't dare stand near for fear of it toppling over) and diversity of produce.

Eating local and organic comes naturally to the people of the Camargue, so it makes sense when Maryse offers to make me a courgette (zucchini) gratin, using what is bounteous in her garden during the summer months. This dish can be found all over the South of France, but I have to say that Maryse's béchamel is the easiest I've ever attempted to make. She whips it up in minutes and there's none of that endless, sweaty sloshing around a hot pot of flour and butter paste that stubbornly refuses to thicken in milk. I don't care what the purists say, I'm all about this garlic-infused, quickie béchamel.

Though baked in a béchamel sauce along with added butter and cheese (the latter of which achieves the all-important golden crust that is essential to a gratin), this courgette bake is light and pairs well with a meatier main or even just a green salad on a summer's day. Ours is, of course, followed by an extravagant cheese board, which I don't hesitate to dive into.

SERVES 4 AS A MAIN OR 6 AS A SIDE

INGREDIENTS

800 g (1 lb 12 oz) courgettes (zucchini), sliced into 5 mm (¼ inch) rounds

40 g (1½ oz) Emmental, finely grated

FOR THE BÉCHAMEL

4 tablespoons plain (all-purpose) flour

390 ml (13 fl oz/1½ cups) whole milk, plus 6 tablespoons

1 tablespoon sunflower oil

2 large garlic cloves, thinly sliced

1½ teaspoons flaky sea salt

4 tablespoons double (heavy) cream

10 g (½ oz) unsalted butter, plus extra for greasing

freshly ground white or black pepper

1. Preheat the oven to 180°C fan (400°F) and generously grease a casserole dish (Dutch oven), or roughly 25 x 32 cm (10 x 13 inch) baking dish or baking tray (pan) with butter.

2. Prepare a steamer or steamer basket over a saucepan of hot water and steam the courgette slices for 6 minutes.

3. Meanwhile, prepare a slurry by combining the flour with 90 ml (3 fl oz/⅓ cup) milk in a small bowl and whisking until smooth.

4. When the courgettes have steamed (they should be slightly softened but still with a bit of bite at this stage), drain them into a colander and leave to steam dry.

5. Heat the sunflower oil in the same saucepan over a low-medium heat and fry the garlic, taking care to stop before it begins to brown. Remove the pan from the heat and leave to cool for a minute, then add the remaining milk to the pan, along with the salt and a grind of white or black pepper, and return to a low-medium heat. Now add the flour and milk mixture and stir like crazy with a wooden spoon for about 5 minutes until you have a smooth and viscous sauce. You don't want a very thick consistency, rather to be pourable like cream. Remove from the heat and add the cream and butter, stirring until combined.

6. Put the courgettes into your chosen baking dish. You don't need to place them delicately and arrange them in layers (though you can if you fancy being fancy!). Maryse just tips them in and shakes the dish to disperse the courgettes evenly. Pour the béchamel sauce over the courgettes and sprinkle over the cheese. Bake in the oven on the top shelf for 25 minutes, or until the gratin is bubbling and golden.

'Like most foods of the peasant people, this courgette gratin was simply born out of an abundance of its key ingredient: courgettes. My parents were farmers from the Camargue. They grew their own vegetables, and we would have so many courgettes in the summer months that my mother practically raised us on this gratin. Some people don't use garlic in this béchamel, or else they use it to flavour it slightly and then take it out. Being from the south, I keep the garlic in.

We southerners are different from the French of the north. We're more open and friendly and tend to be more extroverted. The warmer the weather, the warmer the people. That said, I do believe that the food across all of France is very good. You can't go to a region of France that has terrible food; it doesn't exist. It sounds boastful but that's just the truth.

I've been cooking for 63 years. When I was a young girl, we would be taught by our mothers how to get by in the kitchen, in order to be able to satisfy our future husbands. What I've learned in these six decades in the kitchen is that delicious food really needs a certain dedication of time. It's difficult for young people now to make something truly satisfying because everything's always done in such a rush. The truth is, time is necessary for food to be good; it's an essential pause in the day to treat oneself.

On the subject of time, I also want to impart that while you're young, you should relish and enjoy these days. Don't throw away your years worrying about things that, in the end, matter very little. When you're old like me, you'll find consolation in the beautiful years you spent enjoying your life. If you're not having fun in this moment, change what it is you are doing. Your future self will thank you for it.'

MARYSE — B. 1940 — UZÈS — FRANCE

Maryse's Vinaigrette
Traditional French Salad Dressing

My Italian family are forever rolling their eyes at my need to pair every single dish with a salad. They get a lot of things right over there but my experience of eating in Italy is that fresh greens in the form of salad are always, unfortunately, lacking at the dinner table. The French, on the other hand, know to lift a meal heavy in butter and bounteous amounts of cheese with delicate leaves dressed with finesse.

So basic and yet so intrinsic to French cuisine is the vinaigrette that I can't allow myself to leave Maryse's without her recipe for the ultimate French salad dressing. Drizzle this over rocket (arugula), butterhead (bibb) lettuce, lightly blanched broccoli florets or a selection of herbs and delicate greens. It adds a fragrant and tangy finish to any green salad, that extra *je ne sais quoi* that makes eating salad in France so delectable.

MAKES ENOUGH FOR ONE LEAFY SALAD

INGREDIENTS

1 teaspoon salt

½ teaspoon Dijon mustard

1½ tablespoons good-quality red wine vinegar

5 tablespoons good-quality olive oil

2 garlic cloves, crushed

1. Combine all the ingredients in a large salad bowl and stir together. Just before serving, add your chosen leaves or greens and toss well to coat.

FEASTING

Ninette's Bacalao Escabeche al Fino
Spanish Cod Escabeche

SERVES 6

INGREDIENTS

1 kg (2 lb 4 oz) cod fillet, cut into thick chunks

125 g (4½ oz/1 cup) plain (all-purpose) flour

400 ml (14 fl oz/ generous 1½ cups) olive oil

3 large red onions, sliced into long, thin strips

2 bay leaves

3 garlic cloves, finely chopped

200 g (7 oz) chopped tomatoes (use tinned if you're out of season for fresh!)

60 ml (2 fl oz/¼ cup) tarragon vinegar (white wine vinegar with tarragon extract/ *vinaigre de estragon*)

salt and freshly ground black pepper

In Spain, escabeche is a slightly pickled dish that always involves the use of vinegar. Jaume, Ninette's grandson and chef at the family-run Michelin-star restaurant Béns d'Avall that Ninette founded 60 years ago, insists that her cod escabeche is *al fino* – refined and distinguished, just like this grandmother. This is thanks to the use of a very high-quality vinegar, and just a dash of it.

The result of our afternoon of cooking is an elegant fish dish with the perfect balance of flavours. A confit of onions in vinegar and bay leaves add a sweetness to the fish that demands second helpings.

This is a show-stopper of a dish and surprisingly quick and easy to conjure up. Follow it with her orange and cinnamon (page 210) sorbet at a dinner party.

1. Sprinkle the cod with salt, then spread out the flour on a plate and dip the cod fillets into the flour until lightly coated.

2. Heat the oil in a wide frying pan over a high heat and fry the cod fillets for about 5 minutes, taking care not to turn the fish or poke it too many times as it will fall apart. After 5 minutes, flip the fillets and cook for 5 minutes until golden all over. Gently remove the cod from the pan and place on a plate lined with paper towels.

3. Next, add the onions to the same pan with the leftover oil over a medium heat. Add the bay leaves, ½ tablespoon salt and 1 teaspoon pepper and gently simmer for about 30 minutes until very soft.

4. Meanwhile, combine the tomatoes and garlic in a bowl. When the onions are ready, add the tomato mixture to the onions and cook for a minute or so until the tomatoes and garlic have infused with the onions, then follow up with the vinegar. Cook for a further 5 minutes, then remove from the heat.

5. Place the cod on a serving platter and top with the onion mixture, serving the pimientos asados on the side.

Pimientos Asados

INGREDIENTS

2 red bell peppers

2 green bell peppers

2 yellow bell peppers

1½ tablespoons olive oil, plus extra for drizzling

juice of 1 lemon

1 tablespoon white wine vinegar

1 handful parsley, finely chopped

1. Chop the peppers in half and place inner-pepper side down on a baking tray and pour a generous drizzle of olive oil over them followed by a sprinkling of salt then bake in the oven at 180°C fan (375°F) for 30 minutes until they begin to char. Take them out of the oven once soft and beginning to char in places, place them in a bowl and cover with a tea towel, allowing the skins to begin to steam off.

2. After 10 minutes, peel off any extra skin, chop the pepper into long thin strips then add to a bowl.

3. In a separate bowl, jug or mug, whisk together the lemon juice, the olive oil and the white wine vinegar, followed by the finely chopped parsley.

4. Add your dressing to your peppers and combine well.

'My mother taught me how to make this dish and it's one that I have reverted to again and again because I find it incredibly adaptable. You can eat the cod warm and serve for a family dinner or it can be eaten the next day with a salad. This way, it serves as a good dish throughout the year, as long as you can find the fish, and a good-quality one at that. Another important element of the dish is the vinegar. I use a vinegar that is Chardonnay and very high quality from France, but any good-quality white wine vinegar will work here.

My cooking has an element of finesse because for my most formative years, I lived in France and loved all things French. The food, the culture – all of it was my own for many years before we moved back to Mallorca. My family owned and ran a bar while we lived in France so I was raised with an element of 'Frenchness' that I suppose I have never really shaken.

I have always loved to cook, and I think this is a very important element of putting a meal together. It has to have heart in it. It's one of the things that makes me truly happy, so it made sense to open my own restaurant as an adult. We always worked very hard here, harvesting olive trees and oranges and, at some point in the 1960s, I realised tourists started to arrive to the island and spend time at the beach. My family had a finca very close to the beach people frequented so I opened a little bar of my own there that, at the time, served very simple dishes like pa amb oli and salads but eventually became the family restaurant that is still there today. I would never have thought it would one day be a Michelin-star restaurant. It goes to show what love can bring to a place.'

NINETTE — B. 1935 — MALLORCA — SPAIN

Maja's Crni Rižot
Croatian Cuttlefish Ink Risotto

Maja and I meet in her beachside home just south of the historic town of Sibenik. Her coastal cottage is home to one of the most aesthetically pleasing visions I've ever come across in my decade cooking with grandmothers: Maja, tall and resplendent in a bright green smock dress with elegant red-rimmed glasses that sit at the end of her long nose, framed by a kitchen cabinet and shelves all in the same hue of popping primary red – complete with a Coca-Cola-branded red refrigerator that she tells me is over 60 years old.

Accessories, crockery, cutlery, bread baskets – all of Maja's summer kitchen equipment is red. 'It's my favourite colour,' she says (via a very helpful daughter-in-law who's here translating) and I bob my head up and down emphatically and give her a thumbs up. My Croatian, unfortunately, is limited to *fala* (thank you) and *dobro jutro* (good morning).

When we get to cooking, though, the scents, processes and flavours of the Croatian kitchen are more of a language I can understand. Tossed between the Venetians, Hungarians and Byzantines, this region has been heavily influenced by other cultures in terms of cuisine. The cuttlefish ink risotto I make with Maja is clearly Venetian-inspired, but with a sharp and tangy sweetness that's achieved through the addition of red wine vinegar. The result is a rich dish with great depth of flavour. It's one of those one-pot dishes that I adore for its simplicity, and the colour from the cuttlefish ink adds all the drama.

SERVES 4

INGREDIENTS

1 kg (2 lb 4 oz) cuttlefish, prepared by your fishmonger, with the ink sacs reserved

150 ml (5 fl oz/scant ⅔ cup) olive oil

10 garlic cloves, finely chopped

2 tablespoons finely chopped parsley leaves

1 teaspoon sea salt

½ teaspoon freshly ground black pepper

175 ml (6 fl oz/¾ cup) red wine

1 tablespoon cuttlefish ink (from the reserved sacs, or sachets)

350 g (12 oz/scant 1⅔ cups) arborio rice

400 ml (14 fl oz/generous 1½ cups) boiling water, plus extra as needed

40 ml (1¼ fl oz/2¼ tablespoons) good-quality red wine vinegar

green salad, to serve

1. Buy your cuttlefish from a fishmonger and ask them to prepare it for you, reserving the ink sacs. If you are preparing them yourself, cut or pull away the tentacles from the body, cutting away the beak which will be in the middle of the tentacles. Carefully remove the guts and the ink sac from the main body. Pull out the cuttlebone, then rinse the flesh well, removing any membranes. Be aware, if you're using the ink from the ink sacs you prepare yourself, they are a little fiddly and can dry up if left out too long. The sachets of ink are a great and easy alternative to have as a back up.

2. Before chopping your cuttlefish, set some tentacles aside to decorate the dish at the end. Cuttlefish can vary a lot in size, so if yours are really small keep three whole cuttlefish for decoration instead. Chop the rest into 2 cm (¾ inch) dice.

3. Heat the oil in a large saucepan over a medium-high heat and add the chopped cuttlefish, garlic and 1 tablespoon of the parsley. Cook for 5 minutes, then reduce the heat to low and season with the salt and pepper. Let the pan bubble away for 30 minutes, stirring every so often to make sure it doesn't stick and adding a splash of water if needed (put the lid on if it is spitting too much, but don't forget to keep an eye on it).

4. Next, add the wine, cuttlefish ink and reserved cuttlefish for decoration. Keep the heat on low and simmer for a further 30 minutes.

5. Remove the cuttlefish you'll use for decoration and add the rice, stirring to coat it in the inky, oily sauce. Pour in the boiling water and continue to stir the rice over a low-medium heat for 20–25 minutes, ensuring it doesn't stick to the bottom of the pan, until the rice is al dente. Add a little more water if needed.

6. About 5 minutes before the end of the cooking time, stir in the red wine vinegar – the pop of acidity will lift the dish nicely. Bring to the table with the reserved cuttlefish placed on top and serve with a final sprinkling of fresh parsley, a green salad and a chilled glass of white wine.

'We tend to eat this dish on Christmas Eve alongside fried calamari and octopus as well as cod and potatoes, but there's also another special occasion when we reserve this risotto. Going back many generations, the women of the village would begin to make this when a young woman was going into labour. It's a dish we serve to women who have just given birth. At the time of my mother's youth, more or less everyone was poor, but the coastline provided us with a wealth of seafood. We would make this in order to revive a woman after childbirth and help restore her back to good health.

In the past, babies were born in the home, so there would be a pot of risotto cooking while the labour was still underway. In our culture, we have the tradition of staying at home for 45 days after we give birth, to give the young mother time to gently recover and come to terms with life as a new version of herself. I remember I was treated like a princess after my own birth. The midwives came almost every day and my mother would cook for me and fuss around me with other ladies in the neighbourhood. My only job was to rest and feed the baby.

In those days, it was the midwives who were responsible for birthing children, not doctors. Women helped other women through childbirth and the entire community would pitch in to nurse the young women back to health after their delivery. It was a different time, in which women were given the lead in their own birthing journey.'

MAJA — B. 1947 — SIBENIK — CROATIA

Sitto Sarah's Samak bil-Tahineh
Lebanese Fish in Tahini Sauce

DEDICATION BY CHEF ANISSA HELOU

I had my maternal grandmother in my life well into my thirties. She was a rather imposing figure, not particularly tall, nor heavy, but it was the way she held herself very upright and how she dressed — extremely elegantly, with her hair immaculately gathered into a puffy chignon — that gave her an imperious aura. I loved her and she may have looked commanding, but she was extremely fun to be with, very witty and even catty, never missing a chance to say something mischievously naughty about those who didn't meet her approval. She never sounded malicious, though, mainly because she had an extremely developed sense of humour, always very funny both when she was being kind and when she was being less so.

She was also the most wonderful cook, always preparing our favourite dishes when we visited, which we often did. The recipe below was the last dish I shared with her.

I always think of my grandmother when I prepare this, even if my version is never as good as hers. She would fry the whole fish until the skin was very crisp, before slipping it into the sauce, whereas I use fillets and never manage to have enough of a contrast between the crispy skin and the velvety sauce. We would eat this dish with our hands, picking the fish meat off the bone and scooping it with the tahini sauce using torn pieces of pita — kind of messy but totally delicious. If you prefer to use whole fish like my grandma, use 4–6 small sea bream and be sure to crisp up the skin well before adding them to the tahini sauce.

SERVES 4–6

INGREDIENTS

2 tablespoons pine nuts, or to taste

4 tablespoons extra virgin olive oil

450 g (1 lb) skin-on white fish fillets, such as cod or sea bream, cut into 6 pieces

3 onions, halved and thinly sliced into wedges

1 teaspoon ground cumin

sea salt and ground white pepper

For the tahini sauce

125 ml (4 fl oz/½ cup) tahini

1–2 garlic cloves, finely chopped to a fine paste

juice of 1 lemon, or to taste

200 ml (7 fl oz/scant 1 cup) water

1. Spread out the pine nuts on a non-stick baking sheet and toast in the oven for 5–7 minutes, or until golden brown. Remove from the oven and set aside.

2. Next, make the tahini sauce. Mix the tahini with the garlic in a bowl, then stir in the lemon juice. The tahini will thicken at first, despite the fact that you are adding liquid, but don't let this worry you — it will thin out as you add the water. Slowly add the water, stirring all the time, until the tahini sauce is the consistency of single (light) cream.

3. Heat 1 tablespoon of the olive oil in a non-stick frying pan over a medium-high heat. When the oil is hot, slide in the fish pieces, skin-side down, and cook for about 3 minutes, or until the skin is crisp and golden and the fish is almost cooked through. Transfer to a plate and set aside.

4. Scrape off any bits of fish from the pan, then add the remaining olive oil. Add the onions and cook, stirring occasionally, until soft and very lightly golden. Add the tahini sauce and season with the cumin and a little salt and pepper. Mix well. Let the mixture bubble for a few minutes, stirring every now and then, until you see a little oil rise to the surface. Slide the fish into the sauce. Gently shake the pan back and forth to coat the fish and let the sauce bubble for a couple of minutes, or until the fish is cooked to your liking. Taste and adjusting the seasoning if necessary. Transfer to a serving platter. Scatter the toasted pine nuts all over and serve warm or at room temperature.

Nicoletta's Involtini di Pesce Spada
Sicilian Swordfish Rolls

Nicoletta might well be the lady of an enormous 17th-century palazzo, standing stately on Palermo's promenade, but that doesn't stop her rubbing shoulders with shouty merchants at the Capo market. 'Unfortunately, a modern Duchess doesn't have time to sit around painting her nails,' she tells me as we browse swordfish amid the morning chaos.

I first met Nicoletta years ago when I briefly moved to Palermo. She runs a Sicilian cooking workshop out of the palace in which Lampedusa once sat to write his seminal Italian novel *The Leopard* and I signed up to glean some culinary knowledge of my new home in a remarkable setting.

These swordfish rolls are a go-to for Nicoletta and encapsulate Sicilian cuisine and its complex history. A vibrant burst of citrus and sweet notes from the currants elevates the swordfish while crunchy breadcrumbs and pine nuts add great textural diversity. I like to serve these with Nonna Cece's Insalata di Cedro (page 38), followed by Nonna Carmela's Tiramisu (page 231).

SERVES 4

INGREDIENTS

175 ml (6 fl oz/¾ cup) extra virgin olive oil

1 red onion, finely diced

200 ml (7 fl oz/scant 1 cup) water

160 g (5½ oz) very fine dried breadcrumbs

3 anchovy fillets

1 bunch each of parsley and mint, leaves finely chopped

20 g (¾ oz/ 2 tablespoons) currants

40 g (1½ oz/ 3 tablespoons) pine nuts

zest and juice of 1 lemon

zest and juice of 1 orange, plus 1 orange to serve

1 teaspoon pink peppercorns

1 kg (2 lb 4 oz) swordfish steak, sliced as thinly as possible

15 bay leaves, soaked in water for 10 minutes

2 small onions, quartered

salt and freshly ground black pepper

1. Preheat the oven to 170°C fan (375°F).

2. Heat 50 ml (1¾ fl oz/3½ tablespoons) of the oil in a frying pan over a medium heat and fry the red onion for a minute, then add the water and leave to bubble away for about 15 minutes until the onion is soft and just golden.

3. Once the onion has softened, stir in two thirds of the breadcrumbs and cook for 2–3 minutes to toast them.

4. In a separate bowl, mash the anchovies in another 50 ml (1¾ fl oz/3½ tablespoons) of the olive oil with a fork, then add the herbs, currants, pine nuts, lemon and orange zests and juice and pink peppercorns. Add the toasted breadcrumbs along with a decent crack of black pepper and a pinch of salt. This is what you will use to fill your swordfish slices.

5. Place about 1 teaspoon of the filling on a slice of swordfish, near one of the corners. Roll the corner of the slice over the stuffing, folding and tucking in the edges to keep the same width as you roll the swordfish around the filling, creating a small package. Repeat the process until all the swordfish slices have been used.

6. Thread the swordfish rolls onto wooden skewers, placing a bay leaf and slice of onion between each one. You should manage to fit four rolls per skewer, depending on the length of the skewers you have.

7. Pour the remaining 75 ml (2½ fl oz/5 tablespoons) of olive oil onto a plate and scatter the remaining breadcrumbs over another plate. Dip the swordfish skewers into the oil, turning them to ensure all the rolls are coated in oil, then dipping them into the breadcrumbs.

8. Place the skewers on a baking tray (pan), sprinkle with a final helping of salt and any breadcrumbs that are left on the plate and bake in the oven for 20 minutes, turning the skewers halfway through, until the involtini take on a deep, golden tone.

9. Slice the orange and serve the skewers on top.

'I'm not originally from Sicily and neither was I born into nobility. The Italian aristocracy now is just a title. I didn't marry my husband, Gioacchino, because of a title or because of his palazzo, I married him for the person that he was. There was nearly a 20-year age gap between us but he really was a 'young' person and I loved that. We did a lot together. We moved all over the world because he travelled for his job. He worked as a director of cultural institutes and for a period we lived in New York together where we hosted many dinner parties.

I suppose the art of hosting, including cooking and setting the table, was inherited from my own mother. My parents held a lot of parties when I was a child, and I would help with the preparations. In my adult life with Gioacchino, I continued to play the hostess and, naturally, when we moved to Palermo, the cooking classes began. An American friend of mine insisted on my hosting these in the palazzo after coming to Capo market in the old town with me.

Sicilian food is incredibly rich and regional. It's heavily influenced by those who passed through here and conquered the island throughout various periods of history. We have the Arabs to thank for our inclusion of pine nuts and raisins in many of our recipes, like these swordfish involtini.'

NICOLETTA — B. 1952 — VENICE — ITALY

Luisa's Spaghetti alle Vongole
Neapolitan Fresh Clam Pasta

Nonna Luisa is a proud Napoletana. She lives at the very heart of the city on the coastal road and waxes lyrical about the tomatoes she has sourced for the *spaghetti alle vongole* dish she's cooking with me today. 'This is from Vesuvius, I don't just use any old tomato,' she says, frowning, when I ask her if I might use pomodorini in place of the pointy-ended tomatoes she adds to her *vongole*. When we are ready to add the clams to the dish, I realise that they're still alive in their shells. One pokes its tiny little sucker out of the shell for a second before noticing us and Nonna Lusia starts jiggling it around on the plate, trying – and failing – to get it to come out again. This is how fresh the seafood is in Naples. You buy your clams in the morning at the market and in the afternoon, they're still alive and wistfully searching for the sea.

Spaghetti alle vongole is my favourite of all the pasta dishes this planet has to offer. It is a great privilege to be able to make this dish using Nonna Luisa's recipe because, despite having tried and tested many versions along the Italian coastline, this surely is the best one I've ever had. I adore the added pinch of pepperoncino, a little spice that reflects Nonna Luisa's passionate persona. It takes very little time to make and is an impressive one to serve up for dinner once you master it.

SERVES 4

INGREDIENTS

400 g (14 oz) cherry tomatoes

1 heaped tablespoon sea salt, plus extra to taste

350 g (12 oz) spaghetti

60 ml (2 fl oz/¼ cup) olive oil

4 garlic cloves, halved and germs removed

½ bunch of parsley, stems and leaves separated and leaves finely chopped

2 small dried chillies

850 g (1 lb 14 oz) vongole clams, washed

1. First, make a 1 cm (½ inch) deep incision in the shape of a cross in the top of each tomato, then set aside.

2. Bring a large saucepan of water to the boil for the pasta. Once at a rolling boil, add the salt, then the spaghetti. Make a note of the cooking time on the packet and set a timer for 2 minutes before the end of the suggested cooking – it will finish cooking in the pan with the clams.

3. Meanwhile, heat the oil in a deep frying pan over a low heat and fry the garlic, parsley stems and chillies for 5 minutes, then remove the garlic, parsley and chilli from the pan using a slotted spoon and discard them. Add the tomatoes to the pan, increasing the heat to medium and cover. Allow the tomatoes to steam in their own juices for about 4 minutes, then add the clams, cover again and cook for a minute or so. Add a scant ladle of pasta cooking water to the pan and continue to cook until the clams have opened – discard any that don't. Use a slotted spoon to remove some of the clams and set aside.

4. Drain the pasta, then quickly add it to the pan, stirring constantly until the sauce thickens. Divide between plates and add the reserved clams, plus a sprinkling of parsley leaves. Eat immediately.

'I can't tell you exactly how many years I've been cooking this dish, probably around 60. The key to a good spaghetti alle vongole is to add a lot of oil and the cooking water from the pasta to make sure it doesn't go dry. We're just adding the tomatoes for colour and flavour, rather than to make a sauce, but we still want a silky finish at the end.

Naples is famous for its vongole and we eat a lot of seafood here in the city. We Napolitani are completely mad about food. It is always on our minds and usually the topic of conversation. Sunday lunch with family is a ritual we stick to religiously. It is an excuse to come together, share laughter and a great many dishes. A Neapolitan lunch doesn't just last one hour – sometimes it can go on until dinner time and we will eat and eat and eat and talk about eating while we eat.

Food is an extension of ourselves. How you eat will also affect how you feel. Sharing a meal with family evokes different feelings to dining alone, for example. I think it's important to understand where our food comes from, even more so nowadays. I prefer to buy directly from the producer than go to the supermarket. Naples has some of the best produce in the world. The mozzarella here is incomparable to what you will find anywhere else. We are the food city. Nothing compares to the quality of our food. The clams I'm using for this vongole, they're still alive in their shells, that's how fresh they are.'

LUISA — B. 1943 — SAN GIUSEPPE VESUVIANO — ITALY

Elisa's La Tiella Barese
Oven-baked Potatoes, Rice and Mussels from Bari

In the Italian port town of Bari, nonnas take to the streets to shape orecchiette down the now famous 'pasta alley'. You can walk past their living rooms and see them in there, hands swiftly moving over wooden boards, making pasta on autopilot in front of the television.

Always in search of something a little different, I decided not to track down a pasta alley grandma and head instead to the home of Nonna Elisa, an original inhabitant of the old town who insists that the dish we will cook together is even more Barese than orecchiette pasta.

Patate, riso e cozze (always in this order) is also known as *la tiella Barese* (or *la tiedd* in the Barese dialect), thanks to the traditional terracotta pot it's baked in. Being a port town, Bari is famous for its seafood and this dish, using the mussels that were always plentiful in the region, is no exception. It's a hearty dish – something between a paella and a risotto – that combines layers of potato, rice and mussels, which are then baked in the oven. I find it much handier to throw together than a risotto and far more impressive. Elisa's addition of pecorino makes it all that more substantial and comforting. It's ready when it forms a lovely, golden crust and is best enjoyed with a glass of white wine.

SERVES 4

INGREDIENTS

200 g (7 oz) raw mussels, shells cleaned well with steel wool and rinsed

180 ml (6 fl oz/¾ cup) olive oil

1 onion, roughly sliced into elegant half-moons

½ bunch of parsley, leaves finely chopped

2 garlic cloves, finely chopped

1 x 400 g (14 oz) tin of chopped tomatoes

70 g (2½ oz) pecorino romano, grated

3 large waxy potatoes, peeled and sliced into 7 mm (¼ inch) thick rounds

180 g (6½ oz/generous ¾ cup) arborio rice

225 ml (7½ fl oz/scant 1 cup) water, or as needed

sea salt and freshly ground black pepper

sourdough bread, to serve

1. Preheat the oven to 180°C fan (400°F).

2. Open the mussels by pressing one of the two sides of the shell forward until it cracks open. You can also use a small, sharp knife by inserting it and sliding it until the shell opens. Keep the mussel inside one half of the shell and reserve the water from the mussels in a jug (pitcher) or bowl for later.

3. Use an ovenproof terracotta or ceramic tray (pan) or dish, a cast-iron pan or a small roasting tin that's about 5 cm (2 inches) depth. Drizzle the dish or pan with 2½ tablespoons of the oil then scatter over the onion, followed by 1 tablespoon of the chopped parsley, a sprinkling of salt and pepper and half the garlic. Dot the tray with 2 heaped tablespoons of the chopped tomatoes, followed by 1 tablespoon of the grated pecorino. On top of this, add a layer of the potato slices followed by another 1½ tablespoons of the tomatoes. Now add another tablespoon of parsley and another grind of black pepper, then drizzle with 2½ tablespoons of the olive oil before topping with another tablespoon of grated pecorino.

4. Next up is the rice. Sprinkle half the rice over the dish, followed by another 2 tablespoons of chopped tomatoes, 1 tablespoon of pecorino and a further 2½ tablespoons of olive oil. Now place the mussels on top with the open sides facing up.

5. Sprinkle the remaining rice on top, followed by another scattering of parsley leaves, 2 tablespoons of chopped tomatoes, 1 tablespoon of pecorino and 2½ tablespoons of olive oil. Cover this with a final layer of potatoes, followed by the remaining garlic, tomatoes, more parsley, a sprinkling of salt and a good crack of black pepper, the rest of the pecorino and the remaining olive oil.

6. Pour the water that you set aside from the mussels on top, then add the water until it reaches the bottom layer of potatoes.

7. Place the dish over a medium heat and cook until the water begins to simmer, then transfer to the oven to bake for 50–60 minutes. When it has a nice brown crust and no more water, it's ready to be devoured.

8. Season to taste and serve with good quality sourdough and a crisp glass of Verdeca.

'I grew up with my husband in Bari Vecchia. It's a very rare thing to know your partner for your entire life these days and I am incredibly lucky to have had this gift. He was born in August and I in December, so he has been a permanent fixture in my life since birth. He lived on the floor above ours and as children we would play together. I remember we had a doctor's kit and I would go and fetch the bandages for him to bandage me and my friends up. We were married at 17, which may seem young to some now but it was as though we had already been together for those 17 years. We know each other so deeply and profoundly and love each other through and through. I'm still very happy when I am around him.

Youth has been hard to let go of for me because I was beautiful as a young girl. You should value your youth and beauty and cherish it because the years, inevitably, pass and what you are left with is not quite as pleasing. Still, I have been gifted a good man and a great love and for that, I am grateful.

This dish is a Barese dish, in honour of my Barese man and our Barese love story that began and will end in Bari Vecchia.'

ELISA — B. 1946 — PUGLIA — ITALY

Anastasia's Psiti Tsipoura kai Chorta
Greek Grilled Sea Bream with Wild Greens

My yiayia has not once uttered the words 'I love you' to me. Despite never having heard those three magic words escape her mouth, the ones she does use do a good job of showing me exactly how she feels. 'Have you eaten?' is the sentence yiayia has probably used most in her long life. She's not one for grand shows of affection, choosing instead to subtly express her sentiment through food. When I lived in London and was counting down the days before my next visit to her home in Greece, I would call her up, knowing that she would at some point ask me what I might like to eat on my first day back. This dish in my grandmother's repertoire is the one I would choose every time. Crispy, charred sea bream, aromatic with fennel seeds, dried oregano and citrus is a plate of food that will forever evoke my yiayia.

When it comes to gutting a fish, yiayia prepares hers with great prowess and always with a blunt knife that only she seems to be able to manipulate to great success. She then slips the silver fish onto an old grill grate, years of charring accumulated on its broken bars. She prepares her marinade and dips an entire flower of dried oregano into it, using it to flick olive oil across the fish before sticking the grill over her outhouse kitchen fire at just the right moment to cook the bream to perfection. The addition of fennel seeds is a Corfiot twist, giving the fish the subtle fragrance of anise. My yiayia serves hers with *horta* (wild greens), fried potatoes seasoned with sea salt flakes and oregano and a juicy tomato salad. This is my childhood on a plate. Much more than that, it is an edible manifestation of the uncontainable love my grandmother holds deep inside her.

SERVES 4

INGREDIENTS

4 sea bream, gutted and scaled

2 tablespoons dried oregano

1 tablespoon fennel seeds, lightly crushed in a pestle and mortar

200 ml (7 fl oz/scant 1 cup) olive oil

6 garlic cloves, finely chopped

juice of 1 lemon

flaky sea salt

FOR THE GREENS

1.5 kg (3 lb 5 oz) wild greens (amaranth greens, dandelion greens, beetroot tops or Swiss chard/silverbeet), washed

100 ml (3½ fl oz/scant ½ cup) water

1 wedge of lemon

olive oil

salt

1. With a sharp knife, make 3–4 incisions along each side of the fish, then rub them all over with salt before placing in a large dish.

2. In a bowl, prepare the marinade by combining the oregano, fennel seeds, olive oil and garlic. Take care not to add the lemon juice at this point as it will make the fish stick to the grill. Spoon the marinade over the fish, rubbing the mixture all over and inside the fish to coat.

3. Cook the fish over fire, on a barbecue or under a hot grill (broiler) for 8–10 minutes on each side until the skin is blistered and the fish cooked through.

4. Meanwhile, prepare the wild greens. Heat a splash of olive oil in a saucepan over a medium-high heat and cook the greens until wilted, then add the water, cover, reduce the heat to low leave the greens to steam for 20 minutes.

5. To serve, squeeze the lemon juice over the fish and wild greens just before you serve, along with a sprinkling of salt and extra drizzle of olive oil on the greens.

'It hasn't always been as simple as it is now to eat well on the island. When I was a little girl, we lived under Italian occupation. We were at the mercy of the Germans and Italians that came and stole our homes and our possessions. The Germans took the keys for our home and we were forced to sleep in the small huts that we had built in the olive groves. Corfu in the winter gets damp and very cold, so you can imagine how terrible it was trying to sleep at night. The Italians, at least, were generous and could see that many of us were starving so they would often give us food. They had the generosity of spirit to do that, despite their position in the war. I don't remember being as terrified of the Italians as I was of the Germans, that's for certain.

My memories of those days aren't so clear. I was just a child so, somehow, I pulled through it. It was difficult but most of the days of my childhood were hard. I never went to school and was required to work as soon as it was possible to use a sickle and not hurt myself. My education was in the land. It was raising livestock and planting vegetables and harvesting olives in the pouring rain. I may not be able to write my own name, but I can tell you which wild greens are edible and which herbs will soothe a stomach ache or prevent the onset of a cold.

I didn't really enjoy life until I was married, my children were raised and I could stop working and finally sit down. After raising three children in the village and once they were all married and taken care of, Giorgi (my husband) and I moved to Corfu town. I have to say that these were the best days of my life. I waited 50 years to have a good time. I would clean the house, take my time at the market or spend the day at home cooking and then I would go for a volta [walk] in the afternoons, sometimes out for a coffee. It was a time in which I could finally do what I wanted to do each day. That didn't mean just lazing around, I have always been productive with my time, even now, at 90, I don't sit around doing nothing. Old age is beginning to get to my bones, but I still cook and clean for myself. It's important to have something to do, always.'

ANASTASIA — B. 1937 — CORFU — GREECE

HOTEL SUN

Litsa's Yiouvetsi
Greek Slow Roasted Lamb with Orzo

Like my own Yiayia, Litsa is incapable of sitting still. When I arrive at her home in the historic town of Marathon, she thrusts her homemade chocolates, grape molasses cookies and tea on me while she whizzes around the kitchen. At one point in the process, she conspiratorially links her arm through the nook of mine and takes me through the house, showing me the frill-adorned marital bed she once shared with 'the best husband in the world' before taking me to her current single bedroom, which she has been in since he passed away 30 years ago.

One corner of her room is a shrine to all things Greek Orthodox, from holy wood that she unboxes and insists on me sniffing to iconography and religious literature, some of which she has written and published herself. I'm completely au fait with this corner of a Greek yiayia's house, dedicated to every saint you can imagine. It's a recurring theme across all homes of the octogenarians and nonagenarians of Greece.

Together we cook up a decadent feast of yiouvetsi – roast lamb baked with orzo. Yiouvetsi is the Greek answer to a pasta bake so, of course, we stick a leg of lamb at its heart. This is the crowning glory of any Sunday lunch here in Greece and I have to admit that while my own yiayia's yiouvetsi is a good one, Litsa's is exceptional. She rubs the meat with tomato purée (paste), adding richness and depth of flavour to the crispy outer layer of lamb while the orzo is sauteed in oil, risotto style, before being added to the oven tray to cook in the meat's juices. This prevents the pasta from going mushy and gives it 'bite'.

One important thing to note before you get going with this dish is that, while cooking times are there as a guide, when you take your lamb out of the oven will have a lot to do with the cut and size of the meat and the strength of your oven. Keep an eye on it and don't be afraid to take it out a little sooner or play with the cooking times if you see it's taking on too much colour.

SERVES 8

INGREDIENTS

FOR THE LAMB

3 kg (6 lb 10 oz) lamb on the bone (can be a couple of legs or shoulder – this recipe is very forgiving)

4 large garlic cloves, peeled but left whole

1 tablespoon salt

1 teaspoon ground pepper

1 heaped tablespoon tomato purée (paste)

55 ml (2 fl oz/scant ¼ cup) olive oil

1 large red onion, roughly chopped

3 bay leaves

600 g (1 lb 5 oz) chopped tomatoes

800 ml (27 fl oz/ 3⅓ cups) warm water

FOR THE ORZO

50 ml (1¾ fl oz/ 3½ tablespoons) olive oil

800 g (1 lb 12 oz) orzo

1 teaspoon salt

pinch of freshly ground black pepper

feta and salad, to serve

1. Preheat the oven to 250°C fan (520°F). Using the top and bottom setting rather than the fan for this one as we don't want the lamb to dry out.

2. Place the lamb in a large roasting tin, cutting four deep slices into the bottom of the meat about 3 cm (1¼ inches) apart and stuff the garlic inside. Rub the lamb with the salt, pepper and tomato purée, then drizzle with the olive oil. Tuck the onion and bay leaves underneath the lamb, then roast in the oven for 15 minutes, or until nicely browned.

3. Once the lamb takes on a nice golden hue, remove it from the oven and add the chopped tomatoes to the tin, followed by the water. Reduce the temperature of the oven to 190°C (375°F), cover the tin with a sheet of baking parchment and continue to cook for 1½–2 hours (15–20 minutes per 500 g/1 lb 2 oz of lamb).

4. Twenty minutes before the end of the cooking time, start to prepare the orzo. Heat the oil in a wide pan over a medium heat, then add the orzo, salt and pepper, coating the orzo with the olive oil. Stir constantly for a few minutes, then remove the lamb from the oven, uncover it and pour the orzo into the liquid around it. If you need to, add a splash of boiling water to cover the orzo.

5. Return the roasting tin to the oven, uncovered, and cook for around 10–15 minutes until the orzo has soaked up the lamb juices and cooked to a nice al dente texture. If the lamb has taken on a little too much colour but the orzo still needs more time, add the foil again.

6. Remove from the oven and serve hot with a plate of feta, a fresh and crunchy salad and a splash of village wine.

'I always wanted to be a nursery school teacher because I adore children but I married a butcher and so I ended up working in the butcher's shop alongside him. I was only 17 and I was very much 'married off' to him. Those days were different. If we so much as held hands with a person of the opposite sex we'd be expected to marry them so as not to bring shame on the family. So, we were married, and I had my daughters with him, but he was a tough man to get along with and I was never happy in my first marriage.

I didn't truly find love until I was in my late thirties. That's when I met my second husband. He was a musician and I fell for him when I was old enough to really appreciate his love. He was such a sensitive man. I still have all the beautiful letters he wrote to me. That is what you call passion – it's something we had in common. We were both Aries!

Together we travelled all over Europe and I spent a great deal of time thinking of ways to surprise and delight him. It was a true love, and my friends still tease me about how completely enamoured I was (and still am!) with him. He died 30 years ago but I still feel like a little girl when I think about him.'

LITSA — B. 1937 — EUBOEA — GREECE

Evangelia's Yemista
Rice Filled Summer Vegetables

Though we meet at her 'winter' home in Athens on a bright February day, Yiayia Evangelia chooses to cook a dish with me that sings with all the flavours of a Greek summer, which says a lot about her personality. *Yemista* – meaning 'stuffed' or 'filled' – is a classic traybake that has made its way from the homes of housewives to taverna menus all over the country. Traditionally, tomatoes and green (bell) peppers are filled with herb-spiked rice and roasted in the oven with potatoes.

Being a proud Cretan, Yiayia Evangelia of course gives the tray of *yemista* she cooks with me a distinctly Cretan twist. Dolmades, tiny parcels of rice wrapped in vine leaves, make it into her tray, nestled in among aubergines (eggplants), courgettes (zucchini) and the aforementioned green peppers and tomatoes. She even uses the stuffed vine leaves as a 'cap' for her courgettes and aubergines, stopping any rice from spilling out into the tray.

I'm used to grandmothers using a lot of oil in their food, but I have to award Yiayia Evangelia the prize for most olive oil included in one dish. Her *yemista* required a more than generous 300 ml (10 fl oz/1¼ cups) glug, glug, glug of olive oil. I've cut this in half as I think it works just as well with less.

SERVES 6

INGREDIENTS

1 large onion, roughly choppeds

3 beef (beefsteak) tomatoes

2 courgettes (zucchini)

2 aubergines (eggplants)

3 small-medium green (bell) peppers

2 tablespoons water

500 g (1 lb 2 oz/ generous 2 cups) medium-grain rice, such as karolina, washed and soaked for 30 minutes–3 hours

150 ml (5 fl oz/scant ⅔ cup) extra virgin olive oil, plus extra for the tray

2 tablespoons flaky sea salt

1 teaspoon ground black pepper

½ bunch spearmint, leaves finely chopped

1 heaped tablespoon tomato purée (paste)

20 vine leaves

2 waxy potatoes, peeled and chopped into wedges

1. Preheat the oven to 190°C fan (400°F).
2. Put the chopped onion into a food processor, but don't run it yet.
3. Prepare the tomatoes by slicing off the tops to create lids, then hollowing out the middle, scooping the juice and inner flesh out of the tomato with a spoon to leave about 1 cm (½ inch) of flesh around the outside so that the fruit retains its shape. Put the insides into the food processor with the onion.
4. Prepare the courgettes and aubergines by chopping them in half widthways, then hollowing them out using a vegetable corer – Yiayia Evangelia swears by hers. You can also use a knife and a spoon. Leave 0.5–1 cm (¼–½ inch) of flesh around the outside. You can also use 'bulb' aubergines or courgettes and chop the lids off, then hollow out the middle, as you did the tomatoes. Put the scooped-out courgette and aubergine flesh into the food processor with the onion and tomato.
5. Slice the tops off the peppers, too, and remove the seeds and pith.
6. Now add the water to the food processor and briefly blend the vegetable scraps and onion. taking care to keep a little bit of texture in the mix and not to blend it to a juice.
7. Transfer the blended vegetables to a large bowl along with the drained, soaked rice, olive oil, half the salt, the black pepper, mint and tomato purée. Mix well.
8. Fill the vegetables with the rice mixture and arrange them snuggly in a roasting tin. It's OK for the courgettes and aubergines to be on their sides. Keep mixing the filling as you go to make sure each vegetable gets some of the liquid in the bowl too, as this is important for helping the rice to cook. Put the lids on the tomatoes and peppers. Use the vine leaves to make dolmades, which will be the caps for the courgettes and aubergines. Place a tiny amount (about 1 teaspoon) of leftover filling onto the bottom centre of a vine leaf on the veiny side. Roll up the

leaf, folding in the corners as you go. Once you've used up all the leaves and filling, add the dolmades to the courgettes and aubergines, forming a sort of 'plug' to stop the filling from escaping. Arrange the potato wedges around the stuffed vegetables in the tin.

9. Pour 200 ml (7 fl oz/scant 1 cup) hot water into the bottom of the tin, then drizzle everything with olive oil and sprinkle over the remaining salt. Cover tightly with foil and bake in the oven for 1½ hours, removing the foil for the last 20 minutes. Check the tin during cooking and, if it is looking dry, add a bit more hot water. If your peppers are a bit on the large side, you may want to help them out by adding a splash of water to the filling to help them cook.

10. The vegetables are ready when they begin to brown nicely on top and the rice is cooked in the middle. Cooking times can vary depending on the size of your vegetables, so if you think they need a bit longer, pop the foil back on and leave them in the oven, checking every 10 minutes.

FEASTING

'I'm really a summer person, deep down. Even when it's warm in winter, I tend to turn the heating on and wrap up. I've never been one for cooler climes and even as a child I used to become very irritated when the cooler months rolled around. In Crete, when the season for the tomatoes, courgettes (zucchini) and aubergines (eggplants) is just right at the height of summer, we make yemista, a dish my mother taught me to make nearly 70 years ago.

The traditional way of cooking yemista where I'm from is with vine leaves. We say this is the true flavour of the dish. I make dolmades with vine leaves that I forage with my friends from local vineyards. I still have a group of good friends that I go swimming with or else we head off into nature with our bags to collect vine leaves and other herbs and wild greens that we use in the cooking.

It's important to maintain good relationships, especially as we approach our later years. One of my biggest learnings in life is tolerance. It's no good to take offence to what someone might say in a moment of irrationality or weakness. Each of us never knows what's going on in another person's mind. We should hold things back or else try to understand the other person and their actions. That way, our friendships and other relationships can be tended and looked after. We can't go through life cutting people out when they say something disagreeable. It's so important to cultivate tolerance.'

EVANGELIA — B. 1943 — CRETE — GREECE

Duriye's Bolama
Turkish Beef, Chicken and Chickpea Wishing Stew

SERVES 4

INGREDIENTS

FOR THE STEW

400 g (14 oz) stewing beef, diced

1 chicken breast (about 170 g/6 oz), cubed

100 g (3½ oz) tinned/cooked chickpeas

75 ml (2½ fl oz/5 tablespoons) olive oil

170 g (6 oz) shallots, finely chopped

200 g (7 oz/generous 3/4 cup) passata (sieved tomatoes)

3 tablespoons red pepper paste or tomato purée (paste), or a combination of both

1 teaspoon chopped oregano leaves or dried oregano

1 teaspoon sea salt, plus extra to taste

1 teaspoon freshly ground black pepper, plus extra to taste

FOR THE RICE

300 g (10½ oz/1⅓ cups) short-grain rice, soaked in warm water for at least 1 hour

40 g (1½ oz) short vermicelli pasta (sometimes sold as 'broken vermicelli') or spaghetti, broken into 4 cm (1½ inch) pieces

30 g (1 oz) butter

1 tablespoon olive oil

Duriye is the fourth generation of her maternal family to live in her village in Kuşadasi, and the house we cook in is the home she was born in, just a few doors down from where her great-great-grandmother lived when she was brought to Turkey as a slave from Egypt. The symbolism of the birds Duriye has painted all over her house is not lost on me.

It doesn't take me long to realise that this particular anneanne (grandmother) is a spiritual woman with a deep inner strength. So much has befallen her matrilineal lineage over the course of their history in Turkey but while she acknowledges this and has a keen sense of it, she doesn't let it get in the way of living.

Like many in the region of Izmir, she practices tasseography, the ancient tradition of reading the future in coffee grounds, and her family – many members of which join us to cook – tell me her predictions always come true. She reads my cup and tells me with a dead straight face that I'm going to be famous. Watch this space.

Together, we make *bolama*, an enormous feasting dish that weaves superstition with celebration. This hefty, slow-cooked meat and chickpea (garbanzo) stew originates in the Aegean part of Turkey and involves placing a saucepan of sweet, shallot-infused meat stew upside down in a larger, wider pan and then cooking rice in the stew's juices around the outside. You will therefore need a pan that fits upside down inside another pan to make this.

Traditionally, the matriarchs of the family make *bolama* if they have a wish they would like to realise. They gather the entire family, friends and neighbours to enjoy the meal with them, and everyone eats with the intention of making the particular wish come true. If the wish becomes a reality, the *bolama* is made again as a celebration of the outcome. Duriye says her *bolama* wishes have all come true. We eat ours in her rose and geranium-filled garden. Let's see if mine does...

1. Soak two wooden skewers in water and set aside.

2. Combine all the ingredients for the stew in a bowl and mix well, then transfer to a small heatproof saucepan or dish about 18 cm (7 inches) in diameter and 1.2 litres (40 fl oz/5 cups) volume (a casserole dish, soufflé dish or saucepan with small handles works well). It will need to fit upside down inside a separate wide, high-sided sauté pan or wide, shallow saucepan about 30 cm (12 inches) in diameter so that there is about with 6 cm (2½ inches) or so space around the outside. The stew should fit snugly in the smaller pan or dish – if there is lots of extra space, consider using a smaller pot.

3. Take the soaked wooden skewers and check that they just fit inside the larger pan – cut them down if not. Place the skewers on top of the small pan with the stew inside, one on each side. These will help keep a small gap between the smaller pan and the larger pan, which is important for releasing pressure.

4. Take the larger pan, turn it upside down and place it on top of the small pan. Very carefully turn the whole thing over so that the skewers are now on the bottom with the stew sealed upside down inside the pan. Duriye places a weight on top, like a heatproof jug (pitcher) filled with water, to keep it in place.

5. Cook over a medium-high heat for 5 minutes, then pour 500 ml (17 fl oz/generous 2 cups) water into the gap around the outside of the pan. Reduce the heat to medium and continue to cook for 1 hour, then reduce to medium-low and cook for a further 30 minutes. If it's boiling too ferociously at any point, turn it down to a simmer. You don't want it to boil completely dry and start catching, so if it does, add a little more water.

6. After 1 hour and 30 minutes, remove the pan from the heat for a couple of minutes and wait to see if the upside-down pan releases any more juices. Now, drain the soaked rice and mix it with the vermicelli. Spoon the mixture evenly into the gap around the outside of the smaller pan; there should be just enough juices to cover it, but add a little more water if not. Place back over a medium heat and cook for 5–10 minutes, or until the rice and the pasta are cooked and the juices have been mostly absorbed. Remove the pan from the heat and leave to rest.

7. Meanwhile, melt together the butter and olive oil in a small saucepan over a medium heat. When the small pan has cooled a little, use oven gloves to lift it out from the rice and reveal the stew, then pour the melted butter mixture over the rice and meat and season to taste.

'I was born in this house and I'm the fourth generation of a line of women to live in this village in Kuşadasi. We were originally Egyptian, but my great-grandmother was kidnapped by pirates when she was just 12 years old and brought to the port of Kuşadasi to be sold as a slave. She went to work in a wealthy Ottoman family's home just a few houses up from this one and that's where she gave birth to my grandmother, who I never met.

There's so much generational trauma that exists within my family. My grandmother lost her mother and father young and was adopted as an orphan into the house in which her own mother was kept as a slave. She grew up, married and managed to move out, but her husband was killed in the war while she was pregnant with my mother. Of course, in those days, the man was the sole provider for the family so my grandmother was left with no other choice but to move back to the house of the wealthy family that had kept her mother as a slave. She gave birth there and raised my mother until she was three years old but then tragedy befell the family again and she died of tuberculosis, a disease that was rife during that period here in Turkey.

Like the women that came before her, my mother was left an orphan. Boushranem, the woman whose ancestors had bought her grandmother as a slave, took my mother in and cared for her. She felt an obligation to take care of the many children in the neighbourhood who had been left without their parents. My mother always said that Boushranem was a great woman, but I remember she was a very strict authoritarian that didn't give much away in terms of sentiment.

My grandmother, from whom I get my name, had very few possessions, but from the day of her passing, my mother held tightly onto my grandmother's yemeni – the brightly coloured scarf we use to wrap around our hair. As a child, she would hold it to her nose and sniff it, trying to conjure the scent of her mother. She died in her eighties, still holding that same yemeni to her nose.

All these phases that the women in my family have endured are traumatic but I handle and hold all the pains of my ancestors with love. I cope with all that has happened to the women that came before me by giving love to the women of my future. For now, I'm happy with the few things I have. I'm grateful for the life I was given. I have limited time on this earth, I want to live my days out happily. I don't wonder very much about my future. I'm OK with living in the moment as that's all we ever really have – the here and now.'

DURIYE (DUDU) — B. 1943 — CRETE — GREECE

Bruyère's Frita
Pieds-Noirs Fried Chicken

Upon meeting Mamie Bruyère, I'm reminded of how important cooking can be in the assertion of identity and preservation of culture. She is one of the one million *pieds-noirs*, French citizens who were born in Algeria during the French colonial occupation, which ended in a devastating war in 1962. Expelled by the Algerians from the only homes they knew and unwanted by the mainland French as they flooded into the port city of Marseille, the *pieds-noirs* ('black footed'), as they were pejoratively referred to, had a culinary repertoire that distinguished itself from French cuisine from the very start.

Blending influences from North African, Spanish, Ottoman and Jewish kitchens, the *pieds-noirs* boast dishes that counter the simple flavours that have come to characterise French cuisine. At a time in which views like that of the Mayor of Marseille, who said, *'Que les pieds-noirs aillent se réadapter ailleurs.'* (The refugees had better go somewhere else), the *pieds-noirs* asserted themselves as a new community in France through the food they chose to cook. In defiance of the established French cuisine that Julia Child et al waxed lyrical about, was their kitchen, with harissa, red peppers and couscous being some of its key ingredients.

Matriarchs like Bruyère (now based in Provence) are the ones passing the edible baton on to future generations, maintaining a connection with the home she could never return to and insisting on keeping the memory of her people alive. Naturally, she has chosen to cook me a *pieds-noirs* dish of her mother's: frita. Pan-cooked (bell) peppers with tomatoes are topped with succulent on-the-bone chicken and flavoured with enormous quantities of garlic for a deliciously satisfying sweet and savoury combo.

SERVES 4

INGREDIENTS

150 ml (5 fl oz/scant ⅔ cup) sunflower oil

3 large, ripe beef (beefsteak) tomatoes (about 1 kg/2 lb 4 oz), halved widthways

8 chicken thighs or drumsticks

1 bulb of garlic, cloves thickly sliced

5 large red (bell) peppers, peeled with a peeler and quartered (peeling is optional – Bruyère does this but there are lots of great nutrients in the skin so I leave mine on)

salt and freshly ground black pepper

1. Heat 100 ml (3½ fl oz/scant ½ cup) of the oil in a large, non-stick frying pan over a medium heat, add the tomatoes cut side down and fry for 10–15 minutes, or until they're soft and the skin has wrinkled. Lift them out of the oil and onto a plate to cool.

2. Meanwhile, heat the remaining oil in another large non-stick frying pan over a medium heat and brown the chicken, seasoning with a generous pinch of salt and pepper. Cook for about 15 minutes, using tongs to turn the chicken every 5 minutes, so each side browns nicely. Reduce the heat to low and toss in the garlic, cooking for a further 5 minutes and moving the chicken and garlic round the pan. When the garlic has softened and the chicken is cooked through, turn off the heat and leave in the pan for the flavours to mingle a moment longer.

3. While the chicken sizzles and the tomatoes cool, sauté the peppers with a pinch of salt and pepper in the tomato pan using the same oil, over a medium heat. Turn a few times until they're nice and soft.

4. Once the tomatoes are cool enough, gently peel away their skins and season them with a generous pinch of salt and pepper. Add them back to the pan with the peppers.

5. Remove the chicken pieces to a plate and spoon the garlic into the pan with the peppers and tomatoes. Heat the sauce up again and serve on a platter topped with the chicken.

6. Pair with couscous or, if you're feeling indulgent, with double-fried chips like Bruyère.

'I cook pieds-noirs dishes to recall Algeria and to connect with my culture but mostly, it is in memory of my mother. She was taught this dish by her own mother, who was Spanish. Where we were based, in Mostaganem, there were mainly people of Spanish descent living around us, so the dish probably has a lot of Spanish influence.

When the colonies in Algeria were first established in the 1830s, the French government appealed to French but also to Spanish peasants, offering them their own plots of land in order to get people to move over there and establish a presence. My grandparents were poor farmers from Spain. This is who the pieds-noirs were: normal, working people who were offered a better life. This happened two generations before my own, so I don't know the exact details but, as we know now, this came at the cost of land stolen from the Arabs.

We actually moved back to France 10 years before the war of independence because my parents were rather adventurous and didn't stay in one place for too long. We moved to Morocco for a while before landing in France and then my parents eventually moved to Corsica the year I married, and I followed shortly after. We were never expelled as other members of my family were and so the memories I have of Algeria are fond and not full of the traumas of war and expulsion.

I went back to Algeria for the first time since 1952 just a couple of years ago. Most pieds-noirs people I know never returned because it was too traumatic for them. I went with my brother to find the house we were raised in as children, and it was very emotional for me. The vineyards that I remember from my youth are long gone and when I went to my old home I wasn't well received. An old lady was living there and she became very angry and aggressive towards me, thinking I was there to claim it back. It came as a shock. Another man came out waving the deeds of the house, trying to express in Arabic that it belonged to him. I burst into tears, full of sadness at the situation.

One of the joys of that trip was to make contact again with our Arab neighbours, people I'd grown up with as a little girl. My father was a builder and had worked alongside so many other Arabs. We weren't a rich, bourgeoisie family so, of course, we had many Arab friends that we had left behind. Algeria is where I was born and raised and I'll never forget this.'

BRUYÈRE — B. 1942 — MOSTAGANEM — ALGERIA

Franca's Lasagne

Yes, it's an obvious one, but I couldn't write a book about Mediterranean grandmothers' cuisine without including this Italian nonna staple. Not only is it one of the first dishes a grandmother (that wasn't my own!) shared with me, it's comforting, familial and a recipe I want to pass on to my own daughter, who is half Italian.

I've been sitting on this recipe for almost six years now, ever since my brief escape to Sicily and a short-lived love affair in Palermo. The best thing to come out of that six-month sojourn was the mother of all lasagne recipes, gifted to me by Nonna Franca, who runs an agriturismo at the heart of the island. Within days of meeting the tall, dark handsome man who will not be named, he'd whipped me off to Nonna Franca's, leaving me to follow her around the kitchen while he took part in the annual olive harvest.

Due to the last-minute nature of our trip and the fact I was there for pleasure and not business, I didn't photograph the brilliant Franca or her perfect lasagne. What I did take away was a recipe for the most exquisite lasagne I've ever tasted in my life. Being a carb aficionado, of course I have made, tried and tested other lasagnes, but this one tops them all. I still remember with great pleasure the way Franca artfully drizzled her light béchamel between all the pasta layers, dashing white against bright red *sugo* splatters – a stunning Jackson Pollock of a dish.

SERVES 6–8

INGREDIENTS

750 g (1 lb 10 oz) passata (sieved tomatoes), preferably infused with basil

140 g (5 oz) tomato purée (paste)

300 ml (10 fl oz/1¼ cups) water

4 basil leaves (if the passata doesn't contain basil)

1 bay leaf

50 ml (1¾ fl oz/3½ tablespoons) extra virgin olive oil

2 large white onions, finely diced

500 g (1 lb 2 oz) minced (ground) beef

1 teaspoon salt

½ tsp freshly ground black pepper

16–18 lasagne sheets (about 350 g/12 oz)

40 g (1½ oz) Parmesan, grated

1 ball of mozzarella, sliced

50 g (1¾ oz) unsalted butter, cubed, plus extra for greasing

FOR THE BÉCHAMEL

1 litre (34 fl oz/4¼ cups) milk

70 g (2½ oz) unsalted butter

70 g (2½ oz/generous ½ cup) cornflour (cornstarch)

1 teaspoon salt

½ teaspoon freshly ground black pepper

1. In a wide saucepan, combine the passata, tomato purée and water along with the bayleaf and the basil, if using, and bring to the boil before reducing to a simmer and cooking for 25 minutes until the sauce reduces and thickens.

2. Meanwhile, heat the oil in a frying pan and fry the onions for a couple of minutes until translucent, then tip in the meat and brown for up to 5 minutes. Once the meat has taken on a little colour, add this mixture to the sauce along with the salt and pepper, stirring to combine. Remove from the heat while you prepare the béchamel.

3. Preheat the oven to 180°C fan (400°F).

4. Pour the milk into a saucepan over a medium heat and bring almost to the boil, taking care not to burn it, then transfer it to a jug (pitcher) and rinse the saucepan clean.

5. In the same pan, gently melt the butter over a low-medium heat. Add the cornflour and stir rapidly until it forms a paste and takes on a light biscuit tone. Now gradually pour in the milk, whisking quickly the entire time to ensure no lumps appear. Keep whisking until the béchamel thickens, then add the salt and pepper.

6. Grease a large baking dish with butter, then use a ladle to drizzle a quarter of the béchamel over the bottom of the dish. Now add a quarter of the meat sauce – you can overlap with splodges of red sauce on white béchamel or go checkerboard style and drip the sauce in the empty spaces where there is no béchamel. Use a spatula to spread out the sauce and béchamel layer to the edges of the dish. After this, add a layer of lasagne sheets. You can fill in any gaps with broken lasagne sheets. Repeat the same process with another quarter of the béchamel and sauce, topping with a sprinkling of Parmesan and a third of the mozzarella. Add another layer of lasagne sheets, then repeat the process again until all the sauce and béchamel has been used up. In the end, you should have four layers of béchamel and sauce with three layers of lasagne sheets in between them. The final layer should be topped with the rest of the cheese and the cubed butter, scattered evenly across the top.

7. Bake in the oven for 20 minutes or until golden brown and bubbling on top.

TREATING

Erika's Višnjev Štrudelj
Slovenian Cherry Strudel

I first witnessed Erika make a strudel some years ago now, in a film my good friend Jan Vrhovnik (a very talented director) made in celebration of his grandfather, Eddy. Meeting the duo in person has been something Jan and I have talked about for some time, and it feels as though I already know them by the time Erika shuffles me into her sun-dappled kitchen and Eddy insists on me swigging down cherry schnapps before I even have a chance to have a sip of water.

This cherry strudel is Erika's party piece. She whips it out at family gatherings and the preparation of the strudel is just as enjoyable to partake in as the eating. Erika takes centre stage in the dining room, masterfully spreading her pastry across a cotton-lined table until it is as thin as tracing paper. Once cherries are spread across the pastry, Erika performs like a magician, rolling the strudel into a log with a swift lift and tug of the tablecloth. Blink and you'll miss it. I nearly did.

The result is, for me, a perfect dessert. Satisfyingly crunchy outer layers give way to a gooey, sweet core of cherry lava. Erika serves hers hot, sprinkled with icing (powdered) sugar and frowns at my suggestion of pairing it with anything all. Being half English, I serve mine with warm custard or good-quality vanilla ice cream.

SERVES 10–12

INGREDIENTS

FOR THE PASTRY

600 g (1 lb 5 oz/generous 4¾ cups) T-400 flour (or plain/all-purpose flour), plus extra for dusting

1 teaspoon salt

1 large egg, beaten

80 ml (2¾ fl oz/⅓ cup) sunflower oil, plus extra for greasing

200 ml (7 fl oz/scant 1 cup) lukewarm water, plus extra as needed

FOR THE FILLING

750 g (1 lb 10 oz) cherries (fresh, frozen or tinned), pitted

190 g (6½ oz) caster (superfine) sugar

½ teaspoon vanilla bean paste

1 teaspoon ground cinnamon

4 tablespoons dried breadcrumbs

FOR THE TOP

30 g (1 oz) unsalted butter

icing (powdered) sugar, for dusting

1. Combine the flour and salt in a large bowl, then pour in the beaten egg and oil and mix until it is a sandy texture. A little bit at a time, slowly pour in the water and bring together into a ball. The dough should be fully hydrated but not sticky; if it is too sticky, add a little more flour and if it is dry add a few drops of water.

2. Tip out the dough onto a clean work surface, sprinkle with a little flour and knead for about 10 minutes until smooth. To help develop the gluten, roll it into a rough sausage shape, grab one end and slap the other end hard onto the work surface. Grab the other end and repeat five times.

3. Coat the bottom of the bowl with a little bit of oil, roll the dough back into a ball and place it in the bowl, rolling it in the oil to coat. Cover with a plate or clean, damp dish towel and leave to rest at room temperature for at least 1 hour.

4. Once the dough has rested, preheat the oven to 180°C fan (400°F) and line a large baking sheet with baking parchment.

5. Combine all the filling ingredients except the breadcrumbs in a bowl and set aside. Don't be tempted to do this too far ahead as the fruit will start to macerate and lose a lot of juice. If using frozen cherries, you don't need to defrost them first.

6. Next, prepare to work the dough. Cover a table (roughly 2 x 1.5 metres/6½ x 5 feet) with a cotton tablecloth that you don't mind getting a little greasy and sprinkle flour all over the top. Take the ball of dough out of the bowl and tease it into a flat disc, then place it on a floured surface and use a rolling pin to roll it out to roughly 30 cm (12 inches) in diameter. Place it in the centre of the table. Now stretch the dough very carefully, little by little, until it's paper thin and completely covers the table (a few holes aren't the end of the world, but try to keep them to a minimum). Gently stretch the dough from the inside to the outside, working your way around the sheet of dough. Erika uses a flat, upturned palm to reach under the pastry and stretch it out from underneath, towards her in a stroking motion. Do it in stages, working your way round the table, then go round again, teasing it out a little further each time. Stretch it until it starts to look translucent and you can see the tablecloth through it.

7. Once the pastry is stretched, trim any thicker edges off. Position yourself so that you are standing next to one of the longer sides of the pastry. Sprinkle the breadcrumbs on the lower half of the pastry, followed by the cherries (leaving any juice in the bowl). Fold the left and right side of the pastry in by 5 cm (2 inches) so the filling won't come out at the ends, then lift the bottom edge of the tablecloth and allow the long edge of the pastry to roll down to form a log.

8. Snake the strudel onto the prepared baking sheet, folding it to fit. If you'd like to follow Erika's method, chop the butter into small pieces and dot it all over the top of the strudel. Bake the strudel in the oven for 30–45 minutes until the pastry is golden. Remove from the oven and leave to rest for a few minutes before serving.

'I've lived through tremendous change in my lifetime here in Krško. I survived the Second World War and, not just that, I managed to get out of a concentration camp alive. Before I was born, my family lived here in Krško when the Germans came and rounded everyone up, then took them off to concentration camps. My mother was pregnant with me, but she also had four other children to worry and care for. They were all taken to a concentration camp. We weren't Jewish. The entire family is Christian but still, we were considered a threat to Hitler's regime and didn't fit with the Nazi ideals.

While my mother's four other children died in that camp, I was born. Of the five children my mother brought into the world, I was the only one to survive. As a newborn, I was taken away from my mother by a German nurse so that I could be given a chance at survival. She had probably seen so many children die by that point. Perhaps she felt sorry for my mother, who had suffered so intensely, watching each of her children pass away, one by one.

My mother didn't speak of those times very much but what I have gathered from the little she has shared is that if I had stayed in that camp with her, I would have died. I can't imagine what she must have felt when the nurse took me out of her arms. She had lost so much already.

Even after the war had ended and everyone began to slowly return to their homes to rebuild their lives, my mother and father remained in the camp for months, waiting and hoping for me to be returned to them. It must have been a period of such awful torment, but they waited until the nurse determined I was well enough to travel home to Slovenia with them. It's a trauma that stayed with my mother for the rest of her life, but we were very close and she was an incredibly good person and mother for as long as I knew her.

She lived with us while I raised my children, and I didn't even learn to cook until I was around 40 because my mother was such a great cook that I had never had the need to. In Slovenia, the grandma figure is the matriarch that handles the kitchen so she commandeered mealtimes until she was no longer able to. It was a joint effort, raising my children with her.

This is a traditional Sunday lunch that my mother would make for the whole family and it is very popular here in Slovenia. The meat is always very good in this region and we have always sourced it from our local farmer. Of course, the vegetables are from my garden and have always been something we grow ourselves. I think this is a vestige of Yugoslavia – we didn't have everything readily available as we do now and we did what we could to live a plentiful life. Of course, supermarkets did not exist here at that time and we'd source bread, meat, cheese and milk from a nearby farm. Everything else, we would grow ourselves.

The days of Yugoslavia were really the best period of my life. I think this is the case for many Slovenians. Everything was easier and much simpler than now. We had the possibility to work, we were given a house by the state and it was a safe time for everyone. We had a role in society and we were all on the same financial level. No one was poor and neither were we rich. OK, we didn't have coffee or chocolate, but at least we had a secure roof over our heads, healthcare and education. I had never tasted chocolate or coffee so I didn't care that they weren't available to me, it's not like I could travel across borders and see how people were living elsewhere. I was comfortable. No one was homeless or suffering. That's what really matters, isn't it?

Since 1991 a lot of people have left Slovenia to seek a better life elsewhere. They say 'better' but I'm ambivalent. Is constantly striving for more than what you have and working long hours a 'better' way of living? I am not so sure.'

ERIKA — B. 1945 — KRSKO — SLOVENIA

Tita's Tarta de Limón
Spanish Lemon Tart

When I walk through the gate into Tita's enormous garden, a rogue pony gallops towards me through the lemon trees. This sets the tone for the rest of our morning together, which is spent cooking in her farmhouse kitchen, occasionally interrupted by roaming horses, dogs and the odd family member as we make an exceptionally zingy lemon tart.

This tart only requires the crust to be baked, while the filling is set in the refrigerator. I'm taken by the popping canary-yellow tone the filling takes on once set. Tita insists it's the organic lemons and eggs that she uses that result in such a bold hue. Pleasing also the self-proclaimed 'non-dessert' people out there, this tart is sharper than it is sweet and the perfect palate cleanser, evoking the flavour and feeling of a bright, Spanish spring day.

SERVES 10

INGREDIENTS
FOR THE PASTRY

200 g (7 oz) plain (all-purpose) flour, plus extra for dusting

60 g (2 oz/generous ¼ cup) caster (superfine) sugar

100 g (3½ oz) unsalted butter, plus extra for greasing

1 large egg yolk

2 tablespoons water

FOR THE FILLING

200 ml (7 fl oz/scant 1 cup) lemon juice (from about 4 lemons)

160 g (5½ oz/scant ¾ cup) caster (superfine) sugar

6 medium eggs

1. Grease a 28 cm (11 inch) tart tin (pan).
2. First, make the pastry. Combine all the ingredients in a stand mixer fitted with the paddle attachment and mix until the ingredients come together into a dough, then tip out onto a lightly floured work surface and knead the dough for a minute.
3. Place the dough in the prepared tin, then spread it out and up the sides with your fingertips, ensuring the base and sides are even. The crust will shrink in the oven, so it's a good precaution to have the pastry rise slightly over the sides of the dish.
4. Place the pastry case (shell) in the refrigerator for 30 minutes to chill.
5. Preheat the oven to 190°C fan (400°F).
6. Once the pastry case has chilled, bake it in the oven for 20–25 minutes until golden brown.
7. Meanwhile, prepare the filling. Combine the lemon juice and sugar in a saucepan over a low heat. Crack in the eggs and whisk gently and continuously, taking care not to scramble the eggs. They must cook slowly (up to 10 minutes) and come together like a custard. Set aside once it reaches a custard consistency.
8. Once the crust is golden, remove it from the oven and pour the lemon mixture. Transfer to the refrigerator to chill for at least 30 minutes before serving.

'My mother taught me how to make this tart over 40 years ago and I still make it on a weekly basis. I'm very lucky to always have a full house – I host my neighbours, friends and family every weekend. They always request that I make my lemon tart, and we have plenty of lemons, so I never say no. The key to the filling is to cook it very slowly over a low heat so that the eggs don't scramble. I use the eggs from my own chickens, which I think also adds to its flavour. Good-quality eggs from hens that are happy and free to roam are the only eggs one should eat.

It really is a gift that I live in Sóller. It's a small community and no one is particularly far away. The tunnel that connected Sóller to the rest of the island was only built a couple of decades ago so we've managed to retain a lot of our charm, traditions and customs and we still feel tight as a community. I grew up with my neighbour and we're still good friends. She's here every weekend for the big lunches that I host. The house is never empty and I love that.

There's something incredibly special about living in the Mediterranean. Of course, I've travelled and seen how people live outside of Spain, but the light here is something unrivalled. It gives life to all that grows and touches everything with a beauty that doesn't exist anywhere else.'

TITA — B. 1960 — MALLORCA — SPAIN

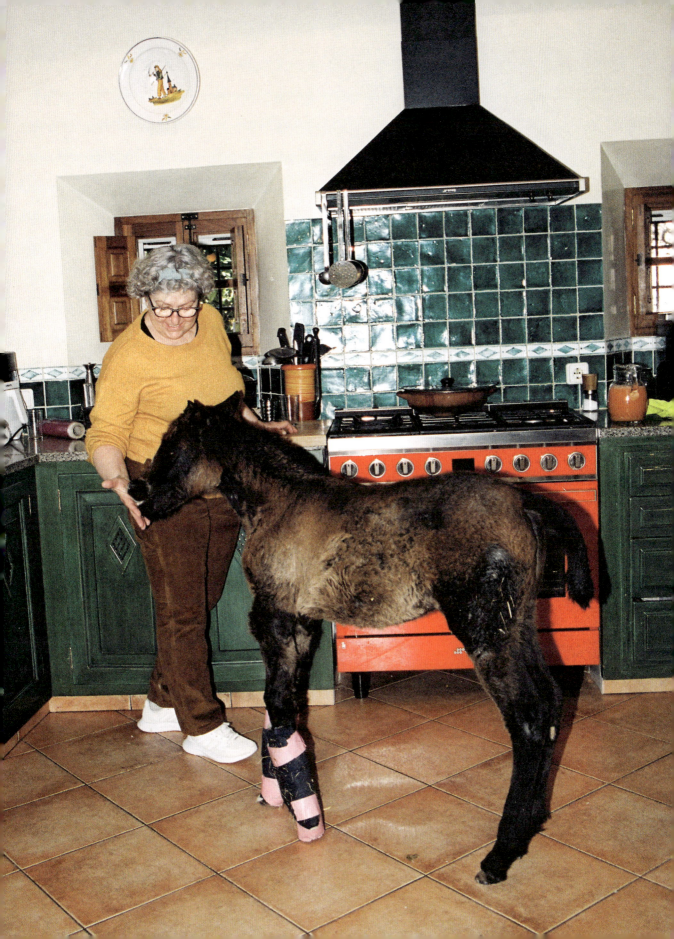

Ninette's Sorbete de Naranja y Canela
Orange and Cinnamon Sorbet

Afternoon golden hour is well into its glorious orange glow as I begin to cook with Ninette in her citrus-surrounded home. Our backdrop is a dramatic mountainscape – I can't have wished for a better location to exemplify the island, or this particular dish, which Ninette tells me is a regular in her repertoire because her grandchildren have always loved it so much.

Her garden is bursting with oranges. Crates are piled high with them and the branches on some of the trees bow down from the weight of the enormous orange baubles, another nod to why this sorbet featured so frequently at her table throughout the years.

To make this sorbet with anything but fresh fruit would be a disservice to this Mallorcan matriarch. Effortless to whip up as a refreshing and palate-cleansing conclusion to Ninette's cod escabeche (page 143), it's a dessert I now return to again and again for a refined (and light) end to an indulgent dinner party.

SERVES 4

INGREDIENTS

150 g (5½ oz) granulated sugar

150 ml (5 fl oz/scant ⅔ cup) water

250 ml (8 fl oz/1 cup) freshly squeezed orange juice (from about 3 oranges)

juice of 1 lemon

1 teaspoon ground cinnamon, plus extra to serve

1 large egg white

50 ml (1¾ fl oz/3½ tablespoons) Cointreau

1. Combine the sugar, water, orange and lemon juice and cinnamon in a saucepan over a low heat and warm gently until the sugar dissolves without allowing the water to boil. Remove from the heat and leave to cool completely.

2. Once the orange mixture has cooled, whisk the egg white in a clean bowl until it forms stiff peaks, then fold the egg white into the orange mixture, followed by the Cointreau.

3. Pour the mixture a container with a lid and freeze. After an hour in the freezer, stir the sorbet with metal spoon. Return the container to the freezer and then repeat the process after another hour. Freeze overnight.

4. Use an ice cream scoop to serve, and finish with a sprinkling of cinnamon.

'When they were still children, my grandchildren adored this dessert. The most simplified version of this is oranges from our orange trees, peeled and sprinkled with a little cinnamon. It's what I would serve them while they were still too young to eat sugar. The sorbet is also very easy to make and I find it more elegant than ice cream at dinner.'

NINETTE — B. 1935 — MALLORCA — SPAIN

Theoni's Galaktoboureko
Greek Semolina Custard Pie

Yiayia Theoni lives in a pretty mountain town on the Greek mainland. On the winding road up to Kalavryta, I pass towering plane trees, and the air gets crisper as I drive closer to her home. Snow-covered Mount Chelmos, which overlooks Kalavryta, looks as though it's been topped with a light sprinkling of sugar, offering an entirely different take on the sun-scorched Greek landscape I am so used to.

While we cook, her age-marked hands trembling as she stirs a bubbling semolina custard, Yiayia Theoni shares with me the devastating history of her town. When she was just 12 years old, Kalavryta was subjected to Greece's biggest massacre during the period of the Second World War. The Holocaust of Kalavryta saw 1,500 men over the age of 14 years old killed by the Nazis in a show of retaliation. Almost the entire male population of the town was exterminated. She bore witness to her home burning down and lost her father and her brother. This trauma has stayed with her all her life.

Together we make a *galaktoboureko*. My dad's favourite dessert of all time and one that will forever remind me of cosy winter mornings at the village *kafeneion*. This custard-filled filo pie has roots in the Balkans, Turkey (*laz böreği*) and, of course, Greece. The crispy outer layers of pastry give way to creamy custard, the ultimate comfort when eaten warm with a dash of orange blossom water in the syrupy coating.

SERVES 9–12

INGREDIENTS

220 g (8 oz) unsalted butter, melted, plus extra for greasing

250 g (9 oz) ready-made filo pastry (about 12 sheets)

FOR THE SYRUP

300 g (10½ oz/scant 1⅓ cups) caster (superfine) sugar

170 ml (6 fl oz/¾ cup) water

1 cinnamon stick

1 lemon wedge or 1 tablespoon orange blossom water

FOR THE CUSTARD

750 ml (25 fl oz/3 cups) whole milk

250 ml (8 fl oz/1 cup) double (heavy) cream

1 vanilla pod (bean), split in half and seeds scraped out

200 g (7 oz/1 cup minus 2 tablespoons) caster (superfine) sugar

90 g (3¼ oz/¾ cup) fine semolina (farina)

30 g (1 oz) unsalted butter

4 large eggs

1. Preheat the oven to 180°C fan (400°F) and grease a 25 x 32 cm (10 x 12½ inch) or similar baking tray (pan) with butter.
2. First, make the syrup. Combine the sugar and water in a saucepan over a medium heat and cook until the sugar dissolves, then add the cinnamon stick and lemon wedge or orange blossom water and bring to the boil. Allow to thicken slightly without stirring, then set aside to cool.
3. For the custard filling, put the milk, cream, vanilla seeds and pod into a saucepan and gently heat over a low heat until you see the first bubbles forming at the edge of the pan. Stir in half the sugar, then slowly add the semolina, stirring constantly. Keep stirring (this is vital to avoid lumps) for 10 minutes, or until the mixture thickens. Remove from the heat, stir in the butter, remove the vanilla pod and set aside to cool slightly.
4. Separate the eggs into two bowls, then add 50 g (1¾ oz/scant ¼ cup) sugar to each bowl. Using a hand mixer, whip the whites for 5 minutes until they form soft peaks, then whip the yolks until fluffy. Now mix the yolks into the whites with a spoon.
5. Give the semolina custard a stir to loosen it, then fold into the fluffy egg mixture until well combined and set aside.

Theoni's Galaktoboureko
Continued

6. Put six layers of filo into the bottom of the prepared tray, using a pastry brush to drip a little of the melted butter over each sheet before adding it (this technique keeps the layers separated during baking, so don't be tempted to brush). Allow the edges of the pastry to hang over so that you can fold them over the custard filling later. This might mean laying one piece centrally and laying subsequent layers shifted slightly over to either side to create more overhang. Work quickly so the filo doesn't dry out.

7. Next, tip the custard filling into the filo-lined tray. You can use a spatula or spoon to spread it out so that it reaches the corners. Fold the overhanging edges of filo over the filling and add another six layers of filo on top, dripping butter between each layer as before. Lay them flat, tucking the edges into the sides or, for a more rustic, textured top, gently scrunch up the filo before opening it out again and laying it on top. Finish with a brush of butter all over, avoiding the white butter solids as these can catch in the oven.

8. Bake in the oven for 25–35 minutes, or until the *galaktoboureko* is golden brown and crispy all over. Remove from the oven and immediately pour over the syrup while it is still hot. Once cooled a little, slice into 12 pieces (or nine if your guests have bigger appetites!). Serve warm or cold, with a Greek coffee.

'Custard will always take a little patience to get right but if you stick with your pot, stir and gently, ever so gently, heat it over a low flame, patience will pay off with a beautiful filling for this pie. Life demands patience. It doesn't always send kind, happy things our way and we need to strive for patience, in order to live with any element of serenity. That is what I have learned, through the devastation that I lived through in my teenage years.

The Holocaust of Kalavryta happened in 1943. I was 12 years old and my house was near destroyed by the Nazis who tore into my town, blood thirsty and full of terrible malice. They burned all the houses in Kalavryta and rounded up all the men, including my father and my brother, Vasilis. He was two years older than me and I idolised him. I remember his calves, how long and strong they were and how much of a man he was growing to be.

Sixteen members of my father's family were killed by the Nazis here. They were taken up to the hill you can see from my window and I remember hearing gunshots. Ear splitting sounds. I was so young I couldn't really comprehend but I remember the terror. Then a woman shouting 'They've killed all our men, they've taken all our men.'

My mother and I ran up there in search of my brother and father. I can't tell you what was going through my mind at the time, just the blood pounding in my ears. Was it not patience that got me through what I was about to see? Corpses. So many of them. My teachers from school. My uncles. My neighbours. The baker, whom I would get my bread from every morning. The town doctor. All of them. We walked through them all. I had blood and brains up to my knees by the time we had found my father and brother. Then – I don't know how we managed this – we took them and buried them ourselves. Imagine, only women and children survived this, and we had no mobile phones to send for help them. It was winter and the snow was falling consistently and our houses were burning down but we took their bodies and buried them, only to find dogs at them the next day.

There are unspeakable things those Nazis did that I cannot even repeat to you now. I will never be able to tell anyone. I wish I could unsee all that I saw that day. The bodies of all of those men. The blood on my hands. Was this not patience? I was so cold by the end of the ordeal that I couldn't stop shivering. My mother begged me to wash the blood from my hands and legs but I was so cold and exhausted I just wanted to sleep. I told her, 'Please mamma, leave me. I just want to sleep.' Waking up to that nightmare and waking every day after it was a lesson in patience. The only thing that pulled me through was a gratitude for my mother and my sister. I was grateful that they had survived with me.'

THEONI — B. 1931 — KALAVRYTA — GREECE

Vasso's Krema Karamele
Crème Caramel

Yiayia Vasso is not your standard Greek yiayia. She is certainly nothing like my own, that's for sure. I arrive to her expansive home on the Athenian Riviera and marvel at the place stacked with antiques she's collected from around the world, crystal and dramatic chandeliers. I understand instantly why she has chosen to make a crème caramel (or krema karamele, as we call it in Greece). She is a refined lady that looks 15 years younger than her 80 plus years. An elegant, smooth dessert suits her just right. Crème caramel is Yiayia Vasso in dessert form.

A wobbly, deliciously creamy flan, crème caramel originated in France but became very popular across European capitals when Vasso was a little girl. Restaurants could prepare it easily in bulk and so the dessert caught on. It's a good option for a dinner party because of how smart it turns out. You can also swap the flavouring, experimenting with orange or lemon zest if you prefer a citrus twist to the vanilla Yiayia Vasso opts for. I like to add a sprinkling of sea salt flakes for a salted caramel kick.

SERVES 6

INGREDIENTS

200 g (7 oz/1 cup minus 2 tablespoons) caster (superfine) sugar

1 tablespoon lemon juice

3 tablespoons water

4 medium eggs

½ teaspoon vanilla bean paste

500 ml (17 fl oz/generous 2 cups) whole milk

flaky sea salt

1. Preheat the oven to 140°C fan (325°F). Put six 150 ml (5 fl oz) ramekins into a high-sided roasting tin and place the tin in the oven so they are warm when the caramel is poured in.

2. Combine half the sugar with the lemon juice and water in a saucepan over a medium heat and leave the mixture to bubble, caramelise and turn golden brown – do not be tempted to stir it. As soon as it reaches a dark copper colour, remove the pan from the heat and quickly pour the caramel into the ramekins, dividing it equally. It will start to harden in a matter of seconds, so be ready. Set the ramekins aside in the tin for later.

3. Next, gently whisk together the eggs, the remaining sugar and the vanilla in a large bowl. Vasso warns not to overwhisk: 'We're not making meringue,' she says.

4. Warm the milk into a saucepan over a low-medium heat, taking care not to let it boil. Once steaming, gradually whisk it into the egg mixture. You don't want it to be piping hot, as that will cook the eggs. Once combined, pour the mixture into the ramekins inside the roasting tin.

5. Carefully pour freshly boiled water into a corner of the tin until the water comes halfway up the ramekins, then cook in the oven for 25–30 minutes, or until the custard has set – the tops should be bouncy. Do not overcook the custard – check around the edges of the dishes to make sure no bubbles are appearing.

6. Remove the tin from the oven and allow the custards to cool down in the water bath. Once cooled, remove the ramekins, cover the tops with foil or cling film (plastic wrap) and pop in the refrigerator overnight.

7. To serve, run a knife around the edge of each ramekin and then place them in a tray of hot water for 1 minute. Place a serving plate on top of the ramekin and flip upside down – it should release, ready to serve. Add a final sprinkle of flaky sea salt for gusto.

'All my children and grandchildren adore this dessert. I've been making it for over 50 years now and it's my mother's recipe. It's very moving how food has the power to bring people together across generations. My own grandchildren eat the same crème caramel that I once did when I was a child. It's quite something, when you think about it. I have a memory of being very small and, together with my siblings, finding a tray of crème caramel that my mother had hidden from us. She knew we were obsessed with it, and she would find new places to hide it so we couldn't get to it before dinner. Of course, we would sometimes discover it and, on this occasion, when we tried to reach it to sneak off with it, but the entire tray came crashing down on top of us, wobbling to a standstill in pieces around us just in time for my mother to rush in and discover us.

Food here in Greece is a source of coming together and I love that. We would have so many parties here. I'd sometimes cater for up to 50 people on our roof terrace and that was a great pleasure for me. Being social and active is woven into our make-up and we Greeks like any excuse for a celebration.

We drink alcohol here at a much younger age, but in this way, we learn to not overdo it. When I was in my early teens, I danced tango, rock and roll and mambo. The 1960s in Athens really were so much fun. At the club, we'd drink vermouth, because that was very 'à la mode' back then, and boys would dance with you and hold you just that little bit tighter dancing the tango if they liked you. It was a time of liberation for women but also of respect. I see now through my granddaughters that society here in Greece has become increasingly macho. We raise our boys in a way that gives them a sense of impunity and it's not a good thing.

I was married at 17 and was pregnant so young. I was told I couldn't have an abortion because it would be damaging and I had to go ahead with the pregnancy. I then went on to separate from my daughter's father because we were really far too young when we married. Of course, we grew apart, it's only natural. Now I say to my granddaughters: don't rush into getting married too young. It's one of my greatest learnings.'

VASSO — B. 1945 — EGYPT (RAISED IN ATHENS)

Ayten's Kalburabasti
Turkish Walnut Biscuits

Ayten lives in the oldest neighbourhood of Kuşadasi, a village in the hills of Turkey's western Aegean coast that burgeoned into a thriving seaside town in the 1980s and now verges on a modern city that sprawls into the hills that Ayten's roof terrace overlooks. Today a cruise destination and busy port, Kuşadasi has transformed completely in Ayten's lifetime. While the cityscape below continues to expand, Ayten's home remains untouched. Her garden is lush with lemon trees, fragrant jasmine is in full bloom and geraniums the tone of paprika explode with colour. We sit in dappled shade to make *kalburabasti*, a celebratory dessert eaten during *bayram* (Turkish days of celebration).

These syrup-soaked biscuits (cookies) are infused with lemon and at their centre sits a little walnut. The dough doesn't contain any sugar and Ayten insists that her ash water (she's been using an ash water mix instead of bicarbonate of soda since time immemorial and obtains her ash from the local bakery) lends to the crunchiness of the finished biscuit.

The slightly knobbly exterior is achieved using a cheese grater to roll the kalburabasti into shape. They're the perfect accompaniment for tea and, contrary to the opinion at Ayten's table, are great served with a scoop of vanilla ice cream.

MAKES 18–20 BISCUITS

INGREDIENTS

FOR THE SYRUP

350 g (12 oz/1½ cups) caster (superfine) sugar

400 ml (14 fl oz/ generous 1½ cups) water

juice of ¼ lemon, plus one thick slice

FOR THE BISCUITS

100 ml (3½ fl oz/scant ½ cup) water

200 ml (7 fl oz/scant 1 cup) olive oil

1 teaspoon bicarbonate of soda (baking soda)

350 g (12 oz/scant 1½ cups) plain (all-purpose) flour

pinch of salt

75 g (2½ oz/¾ cup) walnuts halves, halved again if large

tea and vanilla ice cream, to serve

1. Start by making the syrup. Put the sugar and water into a saucepan over a high heat and heat for about 10 minutes until bubbling and the sugar is fully dissolved. Swirl instead of stirring to avoid sugar crystals forming. Add the lemon juice and slice of lemon and leave to bubble for 3 minutes more, then remove from the heat and allow to cool.

2. Preheat the oven to 200°C fan (425°F) and line a baking sheet with baking parchment.

3. Combine the water and oil in a large bowl. Combine the flour, salt and bicarbonate of soda in a separate bowl. Add the flour mixture to the water and oil in three parts, stirring with a spoon after each addition and then bringing it together with your hands. It should be very soft and malleable but still hold its shape. If your dough is sticky or oily to the touch, you may need to add a dash more flour – knead in a spoonful at a time until the dough loses its oily sheen and becomes more matte in appearance.

4. Once the dough has come together, take walnut-sized pieces (about 25 g/1 oz), roll them into balls and place them on the prepared baking sheet. Repeat with the rest of the dough.

5. Now it's time to create the characteristic knobbles. Take one ball at a time and press it into a flat oval shape (about 3–5 mm/¼ inch thick) against a box grater. Add two walnut halves (quarters, if your walnuts are on the large side) in a horizontal line 1 cm (½ inch) down from the top of the oval. While it is still sitting in the grater, gently fold the dough up over the walnuts on both sides to meet in the middle. Tease it over and press to seal all along, creating a little nugget. Gently roll and peel it off the grater in any direction, trying to keep the knobbles intact. Place on the baking sheet and repeat with the rest of the balls.

6. Bake the finished biscuits in the oven for 20–25 minutes, or until golden brown. Remove from the oven and quickly transfer them to a baking dish or tray (pan) with high sides that they fit fairly snugly into in one layer. Pour the syrup over them while they arere still hot (remove the lemon slice first) and then leave to soak for 20–60 minutes. They should be almost submerged and, if you like, you can flip them over to have a bit of a soak on the other side too. Remove from the syrup and serve with sweet tea and a scoop of ice cream.

'My parents came to Turkey from Crete when they were just children, so our roots were in Greece, long before the republic of Turkey was established in the 1920s and Muslims were asked to abandon their homes on the nearby Greek islands and start a new life here. This recipe was passed on to me by my own mother and she learned it from her mother.

My house is just one street over from the home I was born in and I'm happy to have lived in Kuşadasi in a more tranquil period. When I was a girl, Kuşadasi was made up of these two streets and the rest of the area you now see covered in apartment blocks was tobacco and corn fields. From up here, we had expansive views of all this green around us and the sea. We had animals of course, horses to plough the fields and for basic transport, cows for milk and over 100 chickens.

I was the youngest of five children, so I didn't have many chores growing up. I just remember collecting eggs from the chickens and spending hours running through the fields barefoot. I swear that this connection to the earth, my planting of feet in the soil for so many years as a girl, is the reason I have reached this age. My sister died aged 90. We were grounded and this connection to nature shouldn't ever be underestimated. We were rooted into this place and it kept us alive. Beyond this, a regular afternoon nap always helped with any problem I might have had to face in life.'

AYTEN — B. 1935 — KUŞADASI — TURKEY

Cece's Cassatelle Ragusane
Sicilian Ricotta Tarts

Nonna Cece concludes an epic morning of cooking with her sweet ricotta filled tarts, native to her Sicilian hometown of Ragusa. Ricotta is used across the island in a range of desserts, but these cassatelle are made exclusively here and are not known to every Sicilian, so I feel honoured to be inheriting Cece's generations-old recipe. She uses semolina (farina) in her pastry, which is hardy enough to take wet fillings without the need to par-bake, eliminating the risk of a soggy bottom and making the preparation process a lot simpler. I love the crisp, biscuity crunch of Cece's pastry, perfectly complemented by the smooth ricotta. We eat ours under falling orange blossom so, of course, I've tested my own with a dash of orange blossom water on occasion, attempting to relive a perfectly warm Sicilian spring day with the sweetest nonna. Serve this after Cece's Citron Salad (page 38).

SERVES 6–7

INGREDIENTS

FOR THE PASTRY

125 g (4½/1 cup) hard durum wheat flour (semola rimancicata/fine semolina/farina)

125 g (4½/1 cup) plain (all-purpose) flour, plus extra for dusting

pinch of salt

25 g (1 oz) caster (superfine) sugar

zest of 1 lemon

50 g (1¾ oz) cold unsalted butter or lard, cubed

1 medium egg, beaten

60 ml (2 fl oz/¼ cup) ice-cold water, if needed

FOR THE FILLING

500 g (1 lb 2 oz) ricotta, drained

zest of 1 lemon, plus extra to serve

75 g (2½ oz) caster (superfine) sugar

1 tablespoon lemon juice

1. First, make the pastry. Combine the two flours, the salt, sugar and lemon zest in a large bowl. Add the butter or lard and rub between your fingers until a fine, sandy crumb forms, like you're making a crumble.

2. Add the egg and gently stir through with a wooden spoon – it should start to look like a coarser crumble. If it looks hydrated enough, use your hands to bring the dough together in a squeezing motion (just combine it, don't knead it). If it still looks dry, add the water little by little and bring it together with your hands – it should be firm but not too wet or dry. It's very important not to overwork the dough as you don't want the gluten to overdevelop and the pastry to become tough.

3. Divide the dough into two equal parts and press those into disc shapes. Wrap each one in cling film (plastic wrap) and chill in the refrigerator for 1–2 hours (or you can make it the day before and leave it overnight, like Nonna Cece). If you leave it overnight, remove it from the refrigerator a few minutes before rolling to avoid cracking.

4. When you are ready to make the filling, mix together the ricotta, lemon zest and sugar in a bowl until nice and smooth. Stir in the lemon juice and set aside in the refrigerator.

5. Preheat the oven to 180°C fan (400°F) and line a baking sheet with baking parchment.

6. Take the dough discs out of the refrigerator and roll them out on a lightly floured surface into two large circles, about 2 mm (⅛ inch) thick. Place an upturned bowl (about 14 cm/5½ inches in diameter) on top of the dough and trace around the rim with a knife to cut out circles of dough – you should get at least three per disc of dough (re-roll the offcuts as needed). Place 3½ tablespoons of the ricotta mixture in the middle of each circle, then pinch the sides of the dough together all around the outside to create points – if the dough is not sticking together, use the tiniest amount of water on your finger to bring the sides together and pinch firmly to stop them popping open in the oven. Repeat with the remaining dough.

7. Place the tarts on the prepared baking sheet and bake in the oven on the bottom shelf for 20–25 minutes. After this time has passed, check the bottom is golden, then move onto the top shelf for a final 10 minutes. Remove from the oven and leave to cool, then grate over some more lemon zest before serving.

Carmela's Tiramisù

The dessert to beat all desserts, tiramisu needs little introduction. It has always been my favourite sweet ending to a meal, but when I moved to Sicily a few years ago to learn Italian and realised that tiramisù quite literally means 'pick me up', I fell in love with this dolce all over again.

Carmela's tiramisù is light and creamy. It's less saccharine than others I've tasted across Italy and strikes just the right balance between creamy, sweet and kicky (from the coffee). It's also damn easy to whip up. Don't think about adding alcohol to this one. It isn't traditional tiramisù etiquette and Nonna Carmela would be very upset. She also advises you make it the day before to ensure a tidier slice. She served hers right after her Pasta alla Norma.

SERVES 6

INGREDIENTS

4 large eggs, separated

150 g (5½ oz/scant ⅔ cup) caster (superfine) sugar

500 g (1 lb 2 oz) mascarpone, at room temperature

800 ml (27 fl oz/ 3⅓ cups) brewed espresso (Carmela used 4 coffee pods), cooled

400 g (14 oz) sponge fingers (savoiardi/ ladyfingers; ideally thin ones)

2 tablespoons cocoa (unsweetened) powder

1. Using a hand mixer, whisk the egg whites in a large, clean bowl until soft peaks form. Be careful not to overmix them.
2. Put the egg yolks into a large bowl, add the sugar and whisk until pale and thickened.
3. Gradually add the mascarpone to the yolk and sugar mixture, whisking until combined. Add the egg whites and whisk again briefly until combined.
4. Now make the first layer of sponge fingers. Pour the coffee into a large Tupperware box or small baking dish. Place the dish you will use for your tiramisu next to the dish of coffee – Carmela used a 39 x 17 cm (15 x 7 inch) glass dish, but use any medium-sized deep dish you have. One at a time, dip half the sponge fingers into the dish of cooled coffee very quickly. Make sure this action is in and out in a flash – just as long as it takes to submerge the finger. They should not be soggy at all. Once you've submerged one finger, place it into the tiramisu dish immediately and then repeat the process until half the sponge fingers have been dipped and arranged.
5. Next, spread half the mascarpone mixture onto the sponger fingers. Now repeat the process with the sponge fingers to create another layer of soaked sponge fingers on top of the mascarpone layer. Finally, add the remaining mascarpone mixture and smooth out the top.
6. Place the dish in the refrigerator and chill overnight.
7. Before serving add a thick dusting of sifted cocoa.

'The only downside of tiramisu is that it wasn't invented by Sicilians. It's made all over Italy and we eat it a lot on the island, despite it not being a Sicilian dessert like cannoli or granita. My husband adored tiramisu, so I made it for him frequently. I would whip up a big tray of it and he'd have a slice of it in the afternoons as a merenda. I can see him now, scooping into it with a spoon and smiling at me: 'Carmela, tesoro mio, whatever you make, you make with love,' he'd say.

With him it was love at first sight – and you wouldn't believe that we're from the same island, but we met in the Swiss Alps! I had five brothers growing up and they were so protective of me that I had never been out dancing before until that holiday to Switzerland when I was 18. We were from a small village and there really weren't any places to go to dance. He played the saxophone in a band at a club we went to and from the minute we walked in, I was captivated by him. He asked me to dance that night, and I said no. It's something he teased me about throughout our years together but honestly, I had to say no because I had no idea how to dance.

Making this dish always reminds me of him. He was called Santo, and he truly was a saint by nature. I miss him terribly.'

CARMELA — B. 1940 — MESSINA — SICILY

Marisa's Cassata Siciliana
Sicilian Celebration Cake

SERVES 12

EQUIPMENT

27 cm (10 inch) cake tin; Cassata is traditionally made in a dish with sloping sides and while you can use an ordinary cake tin, I'd advise getting your hands on one with sloping sides as the ricotta has a tendency to collapse the exterior sponge 'walls' of the cassata

rolling pin

metal icing spatula

piping bag with a miniscule nozzle

In the same moment that I find out that Marisa knows how to make a Cassata Siciliana, I book my flights to Sicily. Cassata Siciliana is a lip-lickingly sugared celebration, a dessert to beat all desserts. Chocolate chip spiked ricotta is sandwiched between two layers of sponge, then decorated with green marzipan, an appropriately delicate layer of icing (frosting) and then the crowning glory, candied fruit like precious gemstones sit atop it all. A final flourish comes with an elegant swish, flick or delicate dotting of royal icing.

I adore the Cassata for its more-is-more-is-more feeling. It is how I want to approach my life. In excess. It is all that I love about Sicily and the Sicilian people. It is Dolce & Gabbana in a dessert. I will also add that despite the MEGA amounts of sugar that go into this dish, it isn't cloying. Served cool from the fridge, it is an edible passport to a chaotic Sicilian bar in one bite. Not for everyone, but certainly for me.

The first time I tasted that sweet, smooth, cool ricotta topped in a decadent layer of icing was five years ago, during my first sojourn living in Palermo. I thought my brain might explode. I can safely say that my adoration for Cassata Siciliana has lasted much longer than my Sicilian love affair did. It brings me true joy to know that I can share this original Palermitan recipe with my family for years to come. It's a sweet memory of a moment of absolute hedonism, freedom and indulgence in my twenties – one that I can now relive in greedy mouthfuls, when nostalgia strikes.

Please Note! The cassata requires a couple of days of prep. Take note of refrigeration times and ensure you allow the icing enough time to set before serving. I found having a mug of hot water to hand to dip my metal spatula into very helpful in the icing stage of the process. It loosens the icing which sets quickly and makes it more workable.

PREPARE IN ADVANCE

Sponge Cake Or 'Pan Di Spagna'

Prepare this two days in advance of assembling your cassata. This is a handy recipe to have at hand as it makes a simple, light butterless sponge that can also be used in other desserts like trifle. Contrary to its name, Pan di Spagna is a traditional Italian sponge used as a base for a wide variety of Italian confectionary and leavened with the use of beaten eggs.

INGREDIENTS

6 large eggs

150 g (5 oz) golden caster (superfine) sugar

90 g (3¼ oz/¾ cup) '00' flour

90 g (3¼ oz/¾ cup) cornflour (cornstarch)

zest of ½ lemon

pinch of salt

1. Grease and line a 24 cm (9 inch) cake tin and preheat the oven to 160°C fan (350°F).
2. In a large bowl using a handheld electric whisk or stand mixer, beat the eggs with the sugar for up to 5 minutes until the mixture is pale and almost the consistency of a mousse.
3. Fold in your lemon zest then pour your cake mix into the tin and ensure the top is smooth. Bake in the oven for 45–50 minutes or until golden, then turn onto a wire rack and allow to completely cool. Once it's cool you can wrap it in clingfilm (plastic wrap) and store in a cool dry place until you assemble your cassata.

PREPARE IN ADVANCE

Marzipan

If making your own marzipan, prepare a day in advance of assembling your cassata. Marzipan is fairly easy to make but Marisa shortcuts with a shop-bought marzipan because there are an infinite number of steps in this epic recipe. I'd also advise you do the same but have added a recipe for marzipan below, just in case you're a glutton for punishment like myself and want to try it out.

STORE-BOUGHT OPTION

100 g (5 oz) shop-bought marzipan

1–2 drops of natural green food colouring

1. Knead in the green colouring on a work surface sprinkled with icing sugar. Wrap in clingfilm (plastic wrap) and keep in the fridge until you're ready to assemble.

HOMEMADE OPTION

50 g (2 oz) ground almonds (almond meal)

50 g (2 oz) icing (powdered) sugar

1–2 drops almond extract

1–2 drops liquid food colouring

1 tablespoon water

1. Combine all the ingredients except the water in a large bowl then add a tiny drop of water at a time, using a metal spoon to combine. Don't pour all the water in at once as it may not be necessary and you will finish with a sticky paste rather than a ball of workable marzipan. If your mix is still too wet and sticky, add more sugar and ground almonds, bit by bit until you arrive at a thick dough. Wrap it in clingfilm until you're ready to use it.

'The cassata Siciliana is not only an original dessert of Sicily, it's native to Palermo. The word cassata is actually Arabic, because the Arabs passed through Sicily and gave us much of the food culture that we still hold on to today. They introduced citrus and sugar cane to the island, and candied citrus and sugar have been an essential component in our confectionery ever since.

The 'qas-ah' was the Arabic word for the tin that we use to make the cassata in. I find it ironic because the dish took on a religious connotation and became important within our Catholic festivals. It's eaten during Holy Week and is traditionally consumed on Easter morning. It's been a part of our tradition here since the 10th century, and while of course a version of cassata is made all over Sicily, the true cassata Siciliana belongs to Palermo. The elaborate decoration is Baroque, like our architecture. You can't find it as dramatic or as beautiful in any other part of the island. All the extra flourishes are distinctly Palermitan. I think it is a perfect representation of us in dessert form.'

MARISA — B. 1944 — PALERMO — ITALY

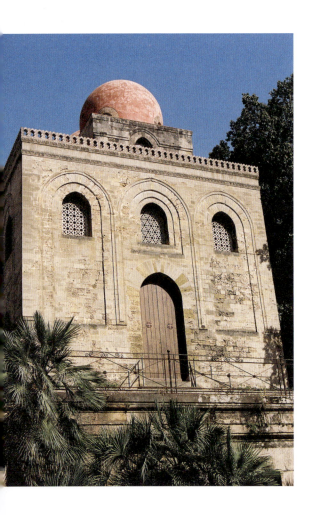

PREPARE IN ADVANCE

Ricotta Cream

Prepare the night before assembling your cassata.

INGREDIENTS

1.25 kg (2 lb 7 oz) sheep's milk ricotta, drained in a sieve overnight using a cheesecloth (muslin)

550 g (1 lb 2 oz) golden caster (superfine) sugar

100 g (4 oz) dark (bittersweet) chocolate, roughly chopped

1. One day before assembling your cassata, drain your ricotta. Place it in a cheesecloth lined sieve, sitting over a large mixing bowl. Use a spatula to gently push the ricotta, which will squeeze some of the moisture out and into the bowl. Cover it in clingfilm (plastic wrap) and leave in the refrigerator overnight to fully drain.

2. The next day, remove the cheesecloth and empty the water that has drained from the bowl and dry it well. Then use the same sieve to push all the ricotta through and into the bowl below, to achieve a smooth consistency.

3. Combine the ricotta with your sugar, using a wooden spoon to mix. Marisa then uses a handheld stick blender on a low setting to achieve a smooth consistency after passing the ricotta through the sieve, eliminating any lurking lumps. Place in the refrigerator while finishing the next steps.

4. Just before assembling the cassata, add your chocolate to the ricotta, stirring it into the mixture so that the chocolate is throughout the cream.

THE DAY OF ASSEMBLY

The 'Bagna' (Soaking Syrup)

Ideally you will assemble the cassata allowing for plenty of time for it to set in the refrigerator before serving. The most practical way of doing this was to begin assembling my cassata in the morning before a dinner party, allowing time to whip up the icing (frosting) and time for the icing to set before decorating with candied fruit.

INGREDIENTS

100 ml (4 fl oz/⅓ cup) water

50 g (2 oz) golden caster (superfine) sugar

4 strips orange zest

2 tablespoons orange blossom water

1. Combine the water, sugar and orange zest in a saucepan and gently bring to a simmer. Ensure the sugar has melted and then remove from the heat. Allow the syrup to cool before adding the orange blossom water and then decant into a spray bottle to use when you're ready to assemble your cassata.

TREATING

THE DAY OF ASSEMBLY

Assembling Your Cassata

Marisa uses a round, 27 cm (10 inch) baking tin with a wider diameter at the top than at the bottom, with sloping sides.

1. Prepare the tin by laying clingfilm (plastic wrap) across the bottom and up the sides of it, leaving enough film at the edges to be able to wrap over the finished layers of sponge inside.

2. Make a template for the marzipan squares that will sit along the circumference of the baking tin using a piece of card or paper. Cut out a square that is the height of the rim of your tin and equal in corresponding width.

3. Sprinkle your work surface and a rolling pin with icing (powdered) sugar and use a rolling pin to roll out your marzipan to 2 mm (⅛ inch) thin and use the template to guide you in scoring out a series of around 10 marzipan squares to line the sides of your tin with. Then line the sides of your tin with your marzipan squares, leaving space in between for an alternating piece of the pre-prepared pan di spagna (sponge).

4. Now for the sponge. Remove from the cake tin and slice off a 1cm thick circle (the 'lid' from the top of the sponge), leaving you with a perfect circle that you can place on the bottom of your cassata tin, which will eventually become the top of your cassata.

5. Take the rest of your pan di spagna and slice it like a loaf of bread, creating 1 cm (½ inch) thick slices of sponge then line around the edges of your tin with these sponge strips which should cover the gaps between the marzipan and also add an extra base to your skinny marzipan squares. Take care to fill any gaps between the sponge at the 'top' of your cassata and the squares along the side with other strips of pan di spagna. Your ricotta will go in the middle and you don't want it to leak through the layers of sponge.

6. Once you've lined the entire tin with sponge, lightly spritz your sponge layer with the pre-prepared 'bagna' in your spray bottle before pouring in your ricotta and chocolate chip interior. Top this with a final layer of pan di spagna, covering every visible bit of ricotta with it before adding a final spritz of the bagna.

7. Wrap tightly using the overhanging clingfilm (plastic wrap) and leave in the refrigerator to set for at least four hours.

The Decor

THE DAY OF ASSEMBLY

INGREDIENTS

360 g (12½ oz) icing (powdered) sugar

5 tablespoons lemon juice

1 tablespoon water

shop-bought candied fruit

1. Unwrap the clingfilm (plastic wrap) layers from the top of the tin then turn out your cassata base by placing a large cake board or plate atop of your tin and inverting.
2. Prepare a metal icing spatula by placing it in a mug of hot water.
3. Weigh out your icing sugar in a large bowl and then add your lemon juice and water a tiny splash at a time, whisking like crazy so that it combines smoothly. Keep adding the water a drop at a time and stir, stir, stir until the icing (frosting) is smooth.
4. Carefully pour the icing atop your cassata, starting in the middle, leaving a little icing aside in case you need to smarten up the sides of the cassata. Use a metal spatula to smooth the icing over the top and then over the sides of the cassata, taking care to move quickly as it dries out and becomes fiddly and unworkable, fast. Keep dipping the palette knife in the hot water to aid the smoothing over process.
5. Place in the refrigerator to set for at least one hour before decorating with the candied fruit and finally, your royal icing.

Royal Icing

THE DAY OF ASSEMBLY

If you've come this far, the royal icing is worth a final few minutes of fuss.

INGREDIENTS

1 egg white

150 g (5½ oz) icing (powdered) sugar

1. In a large bowl, whisk the egg white with the icing sugar using an electric whisk or stand mixer with the beater attachment until it looks like meringue. Then pour into a tiny piping bag with the smallest nozzle you can find and gently pipe a pattern of your choice onto the cassata.
2. Allow the icing to set. And finally, (finally!) serve.

Thank You

A cookbook is the sum of its parts and takes far more than just a great idea or the sheer will of one person to make, especially a book of this nature, which requires an incredible amount of production, pre-planning and the readiness and willingness of other parties to facilitate the cooking process. My first enormous thank you goes to all the grandmothers, their grandchildren and my 'granny dealers', who talked recipes over countless WhatsApp conversations, put up with my broken Spanish, French and Italian and in some cases, put myself and Marco up in their homes (Doga and Kerem, Eddie, Claudia, Mamou – you are always welcome in Greece!). Without your patience, generosity of spirit and hospitality, there would be no book.

Second to that, the talented chefs who took the time to write heartfelt dedications to their grandmothers so that recipes from the countries I couldn't get to were not missed out of this book. I am so pleased we could make it work and hope to visit you in your home country, some day.

Marco, my work wife, chauffeur and supplier of laughs when I have needed them most, it's obvious you're an incredibly talented photographer with great humour, emotional depth and your own punchy style that only gets better as the years tick by. What the world doesn't know is the amount of times you have saved the day with a one-liner, have picked up my spirits when my life has been seemingly falling apart as we drive for five hours on the most sickening Italian highways and how there's absolutely zero judgement when I suggest going to the same Croatian burger chain for the third dinner in a row. You are the OK Mobility of the photographer world. This book is a credit to your talent and to our friendship. *Filakia*.

Jasmine, I cannot count the number of times I have kissed my phone on receiving a WhatsApp message from you detailing the myriad ways in which you have tested a recipe that I could in no way master. The 10-hour baklava really was something and I have you to thank for the precision in many of the baked recipes and for the due diligence that has helped make so many of these time-perfected dishes replicable for any home cook. You're an inspiration and, quite frankly, a wonder. The recipe tester I absolutely could not do this without.

Eve, my editor and part-time therapist. Thank you for putting up with my rants, indignation and frustration. It is such a pleasure to work with someone who has my best interests at heart and truly 'gets' it. I trust you wholeheartedly and honestly marvel at the levels of diplomacy your role requires.

You were really the one that concepted this book and made it a reality for me to publish another celebration of my yiayia, with one of the world's largest publishing houses. I so hope for more video calls with Petala and Calypso.

Elise, it has been such a relief to work with a designer that instantly understands the essence of a project. When you sent over your first cover designs, I was so excited because you seemed to have nailed and completely run with my brief of 'aggressively feminine'. It is punchy, fun and full of colour – the perfect reflection of these matriarchs in a book design.

Manuel, thank you for stepping in with your camera last minute to capture the now famous *cena della cassata*. Not only did you facilitate the finding of that cassata Siciliana recipe but also the final snaps of it too. *Sei un amico bravo e buono, ti voglio un sacco di bene.*

The Blair Partnership, my agents who continue to support my great granny cooking mission and my brand, Matriarch Eats. I so appreciate having some of the best in the business to hold my hand.

Allegra, for offering to help on the cover shoot last minute just because of the stress you saw me under the entire week of our retreat together. You're an excellent cook and stylist and I was so pleased to have your magic touch on those stuffed vegetables, even if yiayia did give an entire tray away before we'd finished the shoot ...

Mini Guide

The below is a note of thanks and a mini guide to where I travelled to and which fantastic hotels and guesthouses were kind enough to host me and Marco on the way, just in case you fancy heading out on your own Mediterranean odyssey.

SPAIN

Jaume and Brooke at Béns d'Avall restaurant, for your brilliant *abuelitas*, the translation when mine and Marco's Spanish was no match for their dialect and for the three sun-soaked days we spent getting to know your beautiful Mallorcan family.

Claudia at Casa Balandra for hosting us in the most beautiful guesthouse and taking us out on the town in Palma, and to Lucia for one of the most memorable 'picky eating' lunches with a view.

Araceli at Antic Mallorca for being so willing to introduce us to Maria and to the wonder that is *pa amb oli*. Also, for weaving wonders with the elderly on the island and preserving Mallorcan crafts and heritage in a way that is so valuable.

ITALY

Davide at Insolito Tour Napoli: Neapolitan tour guide extraordinaire and the man that went the extra mile to source the best nonnas a girl could have wished for. Your powers of diplomacy may well have saved the day.
infotournapoli@gmail.com

Chiara and the family at Magma Home hotel in Naples for hosting us in your stylish central Naples guesthouse. Renata, the best tour guide for eating in Puglia.
italyunseen.com

Raphael at Gaia Felix Winery for an epic Neapolitan family lunch and your glorious biodynamic wines.

Agata, for your enthusiasm and sheer dedication to showing us the best side to Catania and its nonnas.
freetourcatania.com

Alfio at Palazzo Previtera, the most incredible piece of history in a hotel at the foothills of Etna. Your breakfast and your interiors are glorious.
palazzoprevitera.com

AD 1768 Boutique Hotel in Ragusa, for morning views over the piazza.
1768iblahotel.it

Butera 28, for a real palazzo experience of Palermo on the seafront.
butera28.it

TURKEY

Osman and the entire team at Teruar Urla, giving me an alternative taste of Turkey, deep into artichoke land. Your boutique hotel and restaurant are the ultimate way to experience Turkish hospitality and food.
teruarurla.com

FRANCE

Pension Edelweiss in Marseille, a beautiful townhouse hotel at the heart of my new favourite French city.

Boulangerie Pain Pan! Marseille, home to the best pain au chocolat I have ever tasted in my life. You saved the four-hour winding drive through the Provençal hills. Really.

Tuba Club Marseille, for excellent people watching, *fruits de mer* and modernist hotel rooms that have inspired my own interiors.

Regain Marseille – really the best meal we ate in france. Excellent small plates and 'picky eating'.

CROATIA

Mirjana, for a deep dive into the history of Split and excellent local knowledge.
@thestorytellercroatia

SLOVENIA

Hotel April 1550 in Ljubljana, for the sleek and cosy room on a drizzly day and an epic Mediterranean breakfast.

TUNISIA

Lamia at Sawa Taste of Tunisia is really the best person to reach out to for your trip to Tunis. Cooking classes, local history and the most fun trip to the chaotic central market.
sawataste.com

L'Hôtel Particulier La Marsa, for your hospitality and a couscous feast of kingly proportions, you were too kind.

About the Author

Founder of the Matriarch Eats brand, journalist and author Anastasia Miari has been cooking with and interviewing the world's grandmothers for a decade. She holds a Guild of Food Writer's Award for 'inspired storytelling and great journalistic integrity.' Mediterranea is her third cookbook in a series of books dedicated to the lives and kitchens of elderly matriarchs. In her work as a food and travel writer, she freelances for Conde Nast Traveller magazine, Monocle magazine, Konfekt Magazine, Lonely Planet and a number of national newspapers in the UK. Anastasia hosts retreats on her home island of Corfu, giving people a real insight into the worlds of her books.

Index

A

Alfia's *parmigiana di melanzane* 108–9

Algerian pancakes with a thousand holes 32

almonds: marzipan 238

Am Samir's Syrian oozy filo rice parcels 121

Anastasia, Yiayia 72
- Anastasia's *mosharosoupa* 74
- Anastasia's *psiti tsipoura kai chorta* 170

anchovies: Sicilian citron salad 38

Anna's *polpette di ricotta* 104

artichokes: Nezahat's Turkish artichoke and broad bean stew 49

aubergines (eggplants)
- one pan Sicilian aubergine parmigiana 108–9
- Sicilian aubergine tortiglioni 114

Ayten's *kalburabasti* 223

B

bagna 241

beef
- beef and orzo soup 74
- Franca's lasagne 194
- Turkish beef, chicken and chickpea wishing stew 186–7

biscuits, Turkish walnut 223

borlotti (cranberry) beans: Provençal pesto minestrone soup 129

bread
- Mallorcan tomato and olive oil topped sourdough 66
- Palestinian za'atar flatbreads 31

breakfast 20–1
- Turkish breakfast 22–9

broad (fava) beans
- Nezahat's Turkish artichoke and broad bean stew 49
- Pugliese fava with wild chicory 88

Bruyère's *frita* 191

C

cake, Sicilian celebration 235–45

caramel, crème 217

Carmela's *pasta all Norma* 114

Carmela's tiramisù 231

carrot dip, Tunisian 57

cassata 235–45

Cece's *cassatelle ragusane* 226

cedro (citron): Sicilian citron salad 38

cheese
- cheese and herb salad 26
- Franca's lasagne 194
- Maryse's courgette gratin from Camargue 135
- one pan Sicilian aubergine parmigiana 108–9

cherries: Slovenian cherry strudel 200–2

Chiara's *spaghetti all'amatriciana* 101

chicken
- *pieds-noirs* fried chicken 191
- Turkish beef, chicken and chickpea wishing stew 186–7

chickpeas (garbanzos)
- Tunisian chickpea soup 83
- Turkish beef, chicken and chickpea wishing stew 186–7

chicory, Pugliese fava with wild 88

chocolate
- Carmela's tiramisù 231
- ricotta cream 241

cime di rapa, Pugliese pasta with 96–8

cinnamon: orange and cinnamon sorbet 210

clams: Neapolitan fresh clam pasta 161

cod: Spanish cod escabeche 143

coffee: Carmela's tiramisù 231

Concetta's *insalata di Cedro* 38

courgettes (zucchini)
- Cypriot mushroom and courgette risotto with vine leaves 81
- Maryse's courgette gratin from Camargue 135
- rice filled summer vegetables 180–1

crème caramel 217

crisps, red pepper 26

Croatian cuttlefish ink risotto 147

cucina povera 62

currants: Sicilian swordfish rolls 155

custard pie, Greek semolina 212–14

cuttlefish ink risotto, Croatian 147

Cypriot mushroom and courgette risotto with vine leaves 81

D

Dalmatian potato salad 52

dips
- Tunisian carrot dip 57
- yoghurt and garlic dip 26

dressing, traditional French salad 137

dumplings, Turkish yoghurt laced lamb 124–5

Duriye's *bolama* 186–7

E

eggs
- Carmela's tiramisù 231
- eggs on greens 29

Elisa's *la tiella barese* 167

Emmental: Maryse's courgette gratin from Camargue 135

Erika's *višnjev štrudelj* 200–2

escabeche, Spanish cod 143

Esma's *cigar börek* 28

Esma's *cingen pilavi* 26

Esma's *kahvaltı* 22–9

Esma's *kavlama biber* 26

Esma's *otlu yumurta* 29

Evangelia's *yemista* 180–1

F

filo pastry
- Am Samir's Syrian oozy filo rice parcels 121
- Greek semolina custard pie 212–14

fish
- Greek grilled sea bream with wild greens 170
- Lebanese fish in tahini sauce 153
- Sicilian citron salad 38
- Sicilian swordfish rolls 155
- Spanish cod escabeche 143

flatbreads, Palestinian za'atar 31

Franca's lasagne 194

French salad dressing 137

G

garlic
- Croatian cuttlefish ink risotto 147
- *pieds-noirs* fried chicken 191
- yoghurt and garlic dip 26

Giovanna's *fave nette con cicoria matta* 88

gratin: Maryse's courgette gratin from Camargue 135

Greek grilled sea bream with wild greens 170

Greek rice and spinach risotto 77

Greek semolina custard pie 212–14

Greek slow roasted lamb with orzo 175

green beans: Provençal pesto minestrone soup 129

guanciale: Chiara's *spaghetti all'amatriciana* 101

H

herbs: cheese and herb salad 26

Houriye's *omek houria* 57

Index

I

icing, royal 245

Italia's patate *arraganate* 93

J

Jana Lala Hada's Moroccan preserved lemons 60

L

lamb
- Am Samir's Syrian oozy filo rice parcels 121
- Greek slow roasted lamb with orzo 175
- Turkish yoghurt laced lamb dumplings 124–5

Lamia's *baghrir* 32

lasagne, Franca's 194

Latifa's *lablebi* 83

Lebanese fish in tahini sauce 153

lemons
- Jana Lala Hada's Moroccan preserved lemons 60
- Sicilian swordfish rolls 155
- Spanish lemon tart 205

Litsa's *yiouvetsi* 175

Luisa's *spaghetti alle vongole* 161

M

Maja's *crni rižot* 147

Mallorcan tomato and olive oil topped sourdough 66

Mallorcan vegetable tart 45

Margarita's *coca de verduras* 45

Maria Addolorata's *orecchiette con cime di rapa* 96–8

Maria's *pa amb oli* 66

Marisa's *cassata Siciliana* 235

Maryse's courgette gratin from Camargue 135

Maryse's vinaigrette 137

marzipan 238

mascarpone: Carmela's tiramisù 231

Matilda's *krumpir salata* 52

milk: crème caramel 217

minestrone soup, Provençal pesto 129

Moroccan preserved lemons, Jana Lala Hada's 60

mozzarella
- Franca's lasagne 194
- one pan Sicilian aubergine parmigiana 108–9

mushrooms: Cypriot mushroom and courgette risotto with vine leaves 81

mussels: oven-baked potatoes, rice and mussels from Bari 167

N

Napolese oregano baked potatoes 93

Neapolitan fresh clam pasta 161

Nezahat's Turkish artichoke and broad bean stew 49

Nicoletta's *involtini di pesce spada* 155

Ninette's *bacalao escabeche al fino* 143

Ninette's *sorbete de naranja y canela* 210

O

olive oil: Mallorcan tomato and olive oil topped sourdough 66

one pan Sicilian aubergine parmigiana 108–9

oranges
- orange and cinnamon sorbet 210
- Sicilian swordfish rolls 155

oregano: Napolese oregano baked potatoes 93

orzo
- beef and orzo soup 74
- Greek slow roasted lamb with orzo 175

P

Palestinian za'atar flatbreads 31

pan di spagna 238

pancakes: Algerian pancakes with a thousand holes 32

Parmesan: one pan Sicilian aubergine parmigiana 108–9

pasta
- beef and orzo soup 74
- Chiara's *spaghetti all'amatriciana* 101
- Franca's lasagne 194
- Greek slow roasted lamb with orzo 175
- Neapolitan fresh clam pasta 161
- Provençal pesto minestrone soup 129
- Pugliese pasta with cime di rapa 96–8
- Sicilian aubergine tortiglioni 114

peas: Am Samir's Syrian oozy filo rice parcels 121

peppers
- eggs on greens 29
- Mallorcan tomato and olive oil topped sourdough 66
- *pieds-noirs* fried chicken 191
- red pepper crisps with yoghurt and garlic dip 26
- rice filled summer vegetables 180–1

Perihan's *manti* 124–5

pesto: Provençal pesto minestrone soup 129

picky eating 37

pieds-noirs fried chicken 191

pies
- Greek semolina custard pie 212–14
- potato and ricotta filled pies 28

pistou: Provençal pesto minestrone soup 129

potatoes
- Dalmatian potato salad 52
- Napolese oregano baked potatoes 93
- oven-baked potatoes, rice and mussels from Bari 167
- potato and ricotta filled pies 28
- Provençal pesto minestrone soup 129

preserved lemons, Jana Lala Hada's Moroccan 60

Provençal pesto minestrone soup 129

Pugliese fava with wild chicory 88

Pugliese pasta with cime di rapa 96–8

Pugliese ricotta balls in tomato sauce 104

R

red kidney beans: Provençal pesto minestrone soup 129

rice
- Am Samir's Syrian oozy filo rice parcels 121
- Croatian cuttlefish ink risotto 147
- Cypriot mushroom and courgette risotto with vine leaves 81
- Greek rice and spinach risotto 77
- oven-baked potatoes, rice and mussels from Bari 167
- rice filled summer vegetables 180–1
- Turkish beef, chicken and chickpea wishing stew 186–7

ricotta cheese
- potato and ricotta filled pies 28
- Pugliese ricotta balls in tomato sauce 104
- ricotta cream 241
- Sicilian ricotta tarts 226

risotto
- Croatian cuttlefish ink risotto 147
- Cypriot mushroom and courgette risotto with vine leaves 81
- Greek rice and spinach risotto 77

royal icing 245

S

salad dressing, French 137
salads
    cheese and herb salad 26
    Dalmatian potato salad 52
    Sicilian citron salad 38
sea bream: Greek grilled sea bream with wild greens 170
semolina (farina)
    Algerian pancakes with a thousand holes 32
    Greek semolina custard pie 212–14
Sicilian aubergine parmigiana, one pan 108–9
Sicilian aubergine tortiglioni 114
Sicilian celebration cake 235–45
Sicilian citron salad 38
Sicilian ricotta tarts 226
Sicilian swordfish rolls 155
Sitti Malak's *za'atar mana'eesh* 31
Sitto Sarah's *samak bil-tahineh* 153
Slovenian cherry strudel 200–2
soaking syrup 241
sorbet, orange and cinnamon 210
Soula's *spanakorizo* 77
soups
    beef and orzo soup 74
    Provençal pesto minestrone soup 129
    Tunisian chickpea soup 83
sourdough, Mallorcan tomato and olive oil topped 66
spaghetti
    Chiara's *spaghetti all'amatriciana* 101
    Neapolitan fresh clam pasta 161
Spanish cod escabeche 143
Spanish lemon tart 205
spinach: Greek rice and spinach risotto 77
sponge cake 238
sponge fingers: Carmela's tiramisù 231
spring onions (scallions): eggs on greens 29
stews
    Nezahat's Turkish artichoke and broad bean stew 49
    Turkish beef, chicken and chickpea wishing stew 186–7
strudel, Slovenian cherry 200–2
swordfish: Sicilian swordfish rolls 155
Syrian oozy filo rice parcels 121
syrup, soaking 241

T

tahini: Lebanese fish in tahini sauce 153
tarts
    Mallorcan vegetable tart 45
    Sicilian ricotta tarts 226
    Spanish lemon tart 205
Theodoula's deconstructed *koupepia* 81
Theoni's *galaktoboureko* 212–14
tiramisù, Carmela's 231
Tita's *tarta de limón* 205
tomatoes
    Chiara's *spaghetti all'amatriciana* 101
    Franca's lasagne 194
    Greek slow roasted lamb with orzo 175
    Mallorcan tomato and olive oil topped sourdough 66
    Neapolitan fresh clam pasta 161
    one pan Sicilian aubergine parmigiana 108–9
    oven-baked potatoes, rice and mussels from Bari 167
    pieds-noirs fried chicken 191
    Pugliese ricotta balls in tomato sauce 104
    rice filled summer vegetables 180–1
    Sicilian aubergine tortiglioni 114
    Spanish cod escabeche 143
tortiglioni, Sicilian aubergine 114
Tunisian carrot dip 57
Tunisian chickpea soup 83
Turkish beef, chicken and chickpea wishing stew 186–7
Turkish breakfast 22–9
Turkish walnut biscuits 223
Turkish yoghurt laced lamb dumplings 124–5

V

Vasso's *krema karamele* 217
vegetables
    Mallorcan vegetable tart 45
    rice filled summer vegetables 180–1
vinaigrette, Maryse's 137
vine leaves, Cypriot mushroom and courgette risotto with 81

W

walnuts: Turkish walnut biscuits 223
wild greens, Greek grilled sea bream with 170

Y

yoghurt
    Turkish yoghurt laced lamb dumplings 124–5
    yoghurt and garlic dip 26
Yvette's *soupe au pistou* 129

Z

za'atar: Palestinian za'atar flatbreads 31

Quadrille, Penguin Random House UK, One Embassy Gardens, 8 Viaduct Gardens, London SW11 7BW

Quadrille Publishing Limited is part of the Penguin Random House group of companies whose addresses can be found at global.penguinrandomhouse.com

Copyright © Anastasia Miari 2025
Photography ©Marco Argüello 2025

Anastasia Miari has asserted her right to be identified as the author of this Work in accordance with the Copyright, Designs and Patents Act 1988

Penguin Random House values and supports copyright. Copyright fuels creativity, encourages diverse voices, promotes freedom of expression and supports a vibrant culture. Thank you for purchasing an authorised edition of this book and for respecting intellectual property laws by not reproducing, scanning or distributing any part of it by any means without permission. You are supporting authors and enabling Penguin Random House to continue to publish books for everyone.
No part of this book may be used or reproduced in any manner for the purpose of training artificial intelligence technologies or systems. In accordance with Article 4(3) of the DSM Directive 2019/790, Penguin Random House expressly reserves this work from the text and data mining exception.

Published by Quadrille in 2025

www.penguin.co.uk

A CIP catalogue record for this book is available from the British Library

ISBN 978-1-83783-355-9
10 9 8 7 6 5 4 3 2 1

Managing Director, Publishing: Sarah Lavelle
Publishing Director: Kajal Mistry
Senior Commissioning Editor: Eve Marleau
Designers: Elise Santangelo and Double Slice Studio (Amelia Leuzzi & Bonnie Eichelberger)
Photographer: Marco Argüello
Production Director: Stephen Lang
Production Controller: Martina Georgieva

Colour reproduction by p2d

Printed in China by C&C Offset Printing Co., Ltd.

The authorised representative in the EEA is Penguin Random House Ireland, Morrison Chambers, 32 Nassau Street, Dublin D02 YH68.

Penguin Random House is committed to a sustainable future for our business, our readers and our planet. This book is made from Forest Stewardship Council® certified paper.